Four Years
Out of Heaven
Taylor's Story

by Kelly Tumblin

Acknowledgments

First and foremost, I give thanks to God for giving us Taylor and for trusting in us to take care of her for Him.

I thank my husband Roger for always being there: for going the extra miles working; for grocery shopping, and the hundreds of things, large and small, he did to make things easier. I appreciate his ability to put his needs aside for Taylor and me, working incredibly hard just so I could stay home and take care of Taylor. I also thank him for supporting my decision to write this book, *Four Years Out of Heaven*, and for joining me in the hope that someday it will help someone else experiencing the struggles and joys of life with a child born with limitations.

To my daughter Michelle: thank you for always coming when I thought I needed you; for responding to what I considered an emergency—even though it may not have been one. You selflessly shared your priceless healthcare skills and training, patiently teaching me how to give Taylor her meds and treatments. Thank you for taking time out of your own busy life to watch Taylor so I could have some much needed and valuable respite time.

To my son Mitchell: thank you for your gift of humor. You always knew when we needed to laugh and how to bring it about. Thank you for paying attention to what was going on—even when we thought you weren't! And I am so appreciative to you for running errands for me when I couldn't.

To Danielle: I know your life was turned upside down. You weren't expecting a sibling at all. And when Taylor arrived, she wasn't the little sister you thought you would have—one who would pester you, look up to you, follow you around, and get into your things. I hope Taylor taught you what she taught me: that we learn the most and gain strength from our challenges. Taylor knew how to fight health battles like none other and, being her sister, you were just like her when the time came to fight your own. Most of all, I think Taylor taught us the joy of unconditional love.

To my brothers and their families: Mike and Stacy and Allyson, Brady and Abbie: thank you for making long trips to be with Taylor when she needed you. Tim and Janet: thank you for coming all the way here to meet Taylor and for all the support you have given us through all the phone calls to check on her, and on us.

Where do I begin to thank the all the people who supported us in so many ways through Taylor's journey here? Thank you to those who visited Taylor and stayed with us throughout the many, many hospital stays. Thank you family and friends who made countless trips with Taylor and me to doctor appointments in Toledo. To the family, friends, church families, and even people we never met, who prayed for Taylor and for us: thank you. Words of appreciation are all I can give to Taylor's dedicated doctors who went the extra miles to make sure she received all the treatments possible to help her progress. To our hometown EMS for the trips to the hospital and the caring that went along with that, thank you.

And I offer a very special thanks to all the people, including family, friends, our church families, the P. Buckley Moss Foundation (Trees of Life), the Bean Soup Gang, the Oakwood Arbor, and St. Mike's Golf Course, everyone who donated money to help with hospital stays, gas for traveling back and forth, for food and supplies while we were away from home for hospital stays long and short.

I thank my friend Deedi for being Taylor's preschool teacher. You were an incredible support while Taylor was here and after she passed. Thank you especially for editing my book about Taylor's life. To my cousin Beth, thank you for sharing your talents in designing the cover of *Four Years Out of Heaven*, and in record time, too. Thank you, Shelly, for thinking of the winning title for the book—it is a perfect fit. Thanks go to Patti and Lisa for helping me place the photos in the book. Thank you to my Uncle Randy and Diana, Peg, Rhonda, Susie, and Roxanne for helping me when I needed advice about the book. And to all eight of my proofreaders: you have no idea how much you kept me inspired and helped me understand that sharing Taylor's story was something I needed to do. I want to thank Ellie for all the work she did to help the book become a reality. And my newest friend, Georgia, whom I wish could've met and held Taylor. Thank you for all the hard work you put into this book and for showing me the ropes to make it happen. Thanks to Cindy at Baden's Photos for doing a great job on the pictures for this book.

You have all stood by my side and will never know how much we love and care for you. You are all part of Taylor's family.

Family portrait

Foreword

by Dr. Smith

When one is trained in the art of medicine, he or she is taught many different scientific facts about the human condition. This large amount of information, regarding how to detect disease and predict the impact it will have on patients, is part of everyday life for a physician. Sometimes, however, a physician is lucky enough to be educated by a higher power. These educators have not read the book that predicts limitations, handicaps, or expected duration of survival. These educators touch our lives, and give of themselves in ways that many may never truly understand, while teaching us the real meaning of life. For those of us who allow ourselves to be taught this lesson in life, it becomes extremely apparent that we physicians don't know everything and sometimes it's okay to rely on faith and uncertainty. I was blessed to learn this lesson early in my career.

This story is about Taylor, a young lady who I never gave limitations. I often waited for her to show me what she wanted to do, and then I watched her do it. Taylor defied the odds and kept showing the medical field, which had no faith in her, that she would prove them all wrong. She gave a new meaning to the phrase "quality of life." During her short time with her family, she provided them with "unconditional love and quality time." Her visits with me were quite fun, with her always dressed up like a little princess. I have countless pictures of her with the biggest smile on her face and I still glance at them from time to time. Her legacy, left to me, is to teach physicians to care for the patient, not the syndrome or the chromosome abnormality. I am honored to have known her and her family and extremely pleased to have been her advocate and friend. May those parents who read her story seek to find physicians that honor Taylor's legacy.

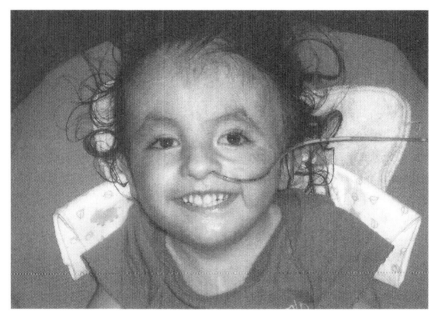

Taylor Tumblin

CHAPTER 1

September 2004

J ust three months after having a tubal reversal, I was pregnant! I was so excited and couldn't wait to tell Roger.

He came home from work and hardly had a chance to sit down before I blurted out the news, "I'm pregnant!"

He looked at me and said, "Already? Are you sure?"

Roger and I have a total of three children from our first marriages. I have two children who are grown and out on their own: a daughter, Michelle, who is a nurse, and a son, Mitchell, who is a machinist. Roger has a teenage daughter, Danielle. This was going to be our baby together. It was September of 2004.

Although I had gotten a positive result with a home pregnancy test, I called to make an appointment with the physician's assistant to be sure.

I went to the clinic and again the pregnancy test was positive. The physician's assistant suggested I see the new obstetrician who had recently started at the clinic. I made the appointment and went to see him. He was so young and very nice. He listened to the baby's heartbeat and it sounded good. The doctor thought I should have a triple screen blood test because of my age—39. The triple screen test measures levels of specific proteins and hormones in the mother's blood, levels that may indicate birth defects including Down syndrome, spina bifida, and Trisomy 18. I agreed to have it done, knowing there wouldn't be a problem. I had two healthy kids. I worked third shift at a factory, felt good, had lots of energy, and considered myself in pretty good shape.

I was told the doctor's office would call me in about two weeks with the results of the blood test. I wasn't worried at all. I was as happy as could be, always smiling and immersed in the excitement of being pregnant; I bought things and began telling everyone about the coming baby.

A week after the blood test, I went home from work and went to bed. Although I needed to sleep, I never turned the phone ringer off because I always felt the kids or Roger might need me. Around 10:00 a.m., the telephone rang.

When I answered, a nurse said, "Kelly, Dr. Winters would like to talk to you. Please hang on."

My immediate thought was, *This can't be good. Why would he want to talk to me personally?*

He came to the phone and his voice cracked when he said, "We got the blood test back. It is not good. The baby tested positive for Trisomy 18. We will run more tests to make sure, because this could be a false positive. We want to be sure."

I sat straight up and asked, "What is Trisomy 18?"

I don't know how many words he used to describe Trisomy 18, but the one I heard was "fatal."

I asked, "Fatal as in death?"

He replied, "Death. I'm sorry."

The doctor assured me there would be more tests done to confirm the findings. The nurse made an appointment at a bigger hospital for an amniocentesis. During this procedure, a large needle is inserted into the womb and amniotic fluid is withdrawn. A specialist would then interpret the results.

The moment I hung up the phone, I jumped out of bed, went to the computer, and typed in Trisomy 18. I started reading and began to cry. The stories and the pictures were so sad. Everything I read was so negative. *This can't be happening*, I thought.

I called my daughter Michelle at work and told her the results and what I was reading.

She said, "Shut the computer off, Mom. Those stories are the worst-case scenarios. Wait to see what the other test reveals."

I just couldn't stop reading and crying. I spent all day and into the evening on the computer. I called into work that night and said I wouldn't be in. I hadn't slept and was in no shape to work.

My mind was working overtime, all the time, constantly wondering what would happen to this precious baby. No matter what I did to try and get it off my mind, I just couldn't stop thinking about it. It felt like a bad dream, but sadly, was very real. Roger, the kids, my family, and friends were very supportive. I couldn't have asked for better love and encouragement. I prayed and prayed and asked everyone I knew to pray that things would work out.

I was 15 weeks along, in my second trimester, when the day arrived for the trip to Toledo for the amniocentesis. Although there was a chance the test could cause a miscarriage, there was nothing else to do. We had no choice. The nurses got everything ready. I was prepped and shortly afterward the doctor came in.

He turned on the ultrasound machine and there was the baby. We could tell by looking that it was a baby.

The doctor said, "It's a girl!"

I looked at Roger. He looked at me and we both smiled. Then I thought, *Please let the other test be wrong.*

Then to our amazement the doctor said, "It looks as though she has six toes." He took a pencil and pointed to each one as he counted, "One, two, three, four, five, and six."

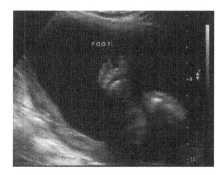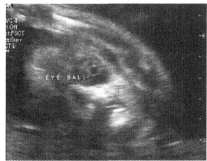

Taylor's ultrasound

I thought, *So what? Six toes, big deal, I can live with that.*

Then he said, "It looks like her feet are on the wrong legs."

I can live with that, I thought again, but at this point I really started to get worried.

Then the doctor looked at us and said, "Her kidneys look deformed. She has no stomach."

I started to cry and asked, "Then how can she still be alive if she doesn't have a stomach?"

He calmly explained that babies don't need a stomach when they are in the womb. Still crying, I realized, despite all my hopes to the contrary, the tests were right. Through my research, I learned that Trisomy 18, also known as Edwards syndrome, is caused by a chromosome defect and typically results in multiple anomalies. Almost all Trisomy 18 infants are born with the same heart defect. They often have rocker-bottom feet, short sternums, low-set ears, cleft palate, cleft lip, clenched hands, and kidney defects with many other deformities possible. They experience severe developmental delays.

I read that these babies have very little movement *in utero*. But, the baby in my womb was never still. I took that as a message from her: "Don't give up on me! I'm fighting and I will keep fighting." The stress of all this was more than I had anticipated and I wasn't sure I could keep it up for nine months. But, if this baby could fight, so could I. And together with Roger, that's exactly what we did.

Chapter 2

January 2005

During all this, my brother Mike stopped by our house one day, came in, and sat on the couch and waited.

I finally asked, "What are you doing?"

He said, "I came to see how the test went in Toledo."

I began to tell him. "Well, it's a girl, but the doctor counted and she has six toes on one foot."

Lightning fast, he said, "So she won't wear open-toed shoes."

I continued, "And they say it looks like her feet are on the wrong legs."

He was ready for that, too, and said, "Kids wear their shoes on the wrong feet all the time."

I went on, "And they said she doesn't have a stomach. They said she doesn't really need it until she's born."

"Then we'll cross that bridge when we get to it."

I have always valued my brother's opinion and that conversation with Mike really stuck in my mind. He was pretty much saying, "Don't give up on this baby." The feet and the toes were not life threatening, and who knew? New medical procedures are discovered every day. I knew then that he and his wife, Stacy, would be a great support for us.

Dr. Winters called me at home a week later with the results from the amniocenteses. He said, "Kelly, the baby has tested positive for Trisomy 18. We will need to get together and discuss what will be done."

We made an appointment just to talk to him about options. One option was an abortion to which Roger and I said, "If God sees fit to take her, He will do it in His time. That is not in our control."

Dr. Winters said, "Whatever your decision is, I will stand behind you 100 percent." And he did. God bless him.

Dr. Winters had a very hard time trying to find a doctor who would agree to deliver the baby. He knew we would need to be at a large hospital where they would have the equipment required to take care of her. . .if she lived. The tragedy of Trisomy 18 is that babies seldom live. Some don't make it to term and are stillborn, some live a few days, some survive to six months, but very few make it to their first birthday. If I had a dime for every time we were told that!

Now the hunt was on for a doctor. No one wanted to take on our case. Many physicians said if I had been an existing patient that would be different. We heard over and over, "These kids just don't live." Finally, Dr. Winters called a doctor from Perrysburg who had trained him during his residency. He agreed to do it and my first appointment with Dr. Wood was scheduled.

My cousin and best friend, Cheryl, went with me. Dr. Wood was a good Christian man, and he treated me so kindly.

All through the visit he kept saying, "Kelly, all we can do is pray. This is a very devastating thing. These kids just don't live. But we can pray and I will pray for you and the baby."

I told him how much we appreciated him taking on our case, and that we were thankful to have a Christian doctor who would not only take care of us physically, but would also pray for us.

Cheryl and I made several trips to Perrysburg to see Dr. Wood. I continued to see Dr. Winters in addition. The baby's heartbeat was always strong. And, contrary to my research, she continued to move so much, at times I could've sworn she was doing somersaults. I often felt a series of continuous jerking movements. I didn't know what they were, but I was glad for all the activity.

I was about five months along when my daughter, Michelle, came to me and said, "Don't tell anyone, but I'm pregnant."

I was excited for her and for us. Our baby would have a playmate. This was something positive to start thinking about, instead of all the negative stuff. I had no idea at the time how badly Michelle felt about all that was going wrong with my pregnancy.

When I told her about my doctor visits, she would get very quiet and often say, "Mom, I'm so sorry you are going through this."

I said, "Don't ever say you're sorry. We will get through this. God has a plan. I just know He does."

I worked with a guy who was a lot of fun. When I was about five months along, I told him we were having a girl and needed to pick out a name. All night as we worked, I kept saying baby names to which he would reply, "No way. No way."

Finally I said, "Taylor Tumblin. I can just hear it now. 'An–n–nd Taylor Tumblin goes for the shot and she makes it!'"

He said, "You're crazy."

"It has to be Taylor," I replied.

When I got home from work that morning and talked to Roger about my choice of names, he said that it sounded good to him. Now our baby had a name. Taylor.

† Chapter 3 †

May 2005

I was invited by my friend from the factory where I worked, Val, to go to a revival at her church. The woman holding the service prayed for people with specific needs, and we needed all the prayers we could get.

When it came time to go forward, I was scared but Val went with me. The minister put her hand on the forehead of the person being prayed for. I had been to churches where they did this, but never had experienced it until then. It always looked to me like they pushed people down. That wasn't how it was at all. I was actually on the floor before I knew what was happening.

She preached in a language I understood. She later told my friend, Val, when she laid her hands on me she could see a little girl in a dress playing with other kids. This became another positive for me to focus on, and I did. Her sermon touched me like no other and I felt a lot better about things after that day.

I continued researching Trisomy 18 and learned that one out of every 3,000 babies is born with Trisomy 18, and of those, less than 10 percent live to see a first birthday. Fifty percent will carry to term, but are stillborn. I also learned that Trisomy 18 boys have a higher rate of stillbirth than girls.

My friends at the factory were so positive about everything. They even had a baby shower for me. They told me they were going to have it during lunch. I suggested waiting until the baby was born, but they responded, "No way! Taylor will need this stuff when she comes home."

Sometimes my spirits were low, but friends like that and my family helped to lift me back up again. Unfortunately, not all people were that encouraging. At work I heard so many rude remarks, plus some people reported to me what others had said. This didn't happen just at the factory; there were other instances. The people who made such mean and hurtful statements weren't really a part of our lives. Since they wouldn't have any involvement, their opinion didn't mean anything. Roger and I were depending on God. All the love and support from our family and friends was just an extra blessing.

The shower went on as planned and we couldn't believe the number of gifts we received: a high chair, Pack-n-Play bed, clothing, baby books, and picture frames, just to name a few things. These good people stood behind us in every way. They didn't want Taylor to want for anything, and she didn't.

Throughout my pregnancy, Dr. Winters continued to order ultrasounds almost every month. I tried to figure out what I was seeing on the screen.

At Taylor's baby shower

One time the ultrasound technician and I were talking and I said, "They told us in Toledo she doesn't have a stomach and we saw six toes on one foot."

The tech was silent for a moment and then said, "Kelly, you know I'm not supposed to tell you anything I see."

But she pointed to the screen and said, "Here is her stomach."

On the screen, Taylor's feet looked like they were flat, not curved like rocker-bottom feet.

The tech took photos and pointed out first one and then the other of Taylor's feet.

"Here are five toes and here are five toes."

The foot on which we had previously counted six toes, now had only five. Roger and I had seen and counted six toes on that first ultrasound. But now it appeared that only a space, not a sixth toe was in between her big toe and the next! I am still amazed every time I look at the ultrasound of her feet from that day.

The tech continued the ultrasound and said, "The kidneys are here. They look a little deformed but the main shape is there."

By then, I couldn't stop crying from the news. It was great! Maybe all the other theories were wrong, too. No matter what, our baby was a fighter, and a miracle!

Dr. Wood told us that she should be delivered by C-section at 39 weeks, so we decided that Taylor would be born June 9, 2005. We prayed every day she would make it to term without complications.

It was about two weeks before Taylor's due date and we had to get her bedroom ready. My cousin Peg and I painted her room light pink on the bottom and white on top. In the middle we added a Care Bears border. It was very cute, but I sure paid for it the next day. While we were working on the nursery, Peg told me to take it easy and not to climb the ladder, but I'm hardheaded and did it anyway.

The next morning when I tried to get out of bed, I had double vision. The room whirled around me. If I opened my eyes, I threw up. Roger called my cousin Cheryl. She came right over and called Dr. Winters who told her to get me to the hospital. He said he would call the doctor on duty and tell him I was on my way and what was going on. Cheryl came along. Roger drove as fast as he could. I couldn't open my eyes or things started spinning and I would get sick.

When we arrived at the hospital, it was obvious the hospital staff was not comfortable with me there. They were afraid I was going to deliver Taylor at their facility before I could be transferred and that was the last thing they wanted. I was put in a room by myself and left alone. I think they went out in the hall and just wished I would disappear. Roger had returned home to pack bags because I was supposed to be sent to Toledo from Defiance. Cheryl went to run some errands.

Although the door to my room was shut, I hadn't been given a "call nurse button." I was so sick I couldn't get out of bed, let alone walk to the bathroom. I yelled for help, but no one came. I vomited all over the bed and myself. Still, no one came. When Cheryl came back, she found me crying, a mess, and very sick. She was furious and marched right out to the nurses' station, got someone and brought her into the room.

"Why wouldn't you guys help her?" Cheryl demanded.

The answer: "We didn't hear her."

"Of course you didn't hear her!" Cheryl said. "The door was shut and you didn't give her a call button!"

Finally the ambulance came to pick me up and take me to the hospital in Toledo. Roger and Cheryl followed in the car. All the way there I continued to be terribly sick. After what seemed a lifetime, we finally arrived.

The first thing I was asked was, "What level is your pain?"

"I am not in pain," I said. "I'm sick."

They thought I was in labor because the staff at the first hospital wanted me out of there so badly, they told the larger hospital that I was in labor.

I was hooked up to machines to monitor the baby and try to diagnose what was going on. It was then I learned that all the jerking the baby had been doing was hiccups. That was the best news I could've received. What a relief!

Dr. Wood, the doctor from Perrysburg, came in. He said, "I say we deliver this baby so you can hold her while she's alive."

He knew she would only live a few hours after birth.

Roger had left because for months we'd had tickets to the drag races in Columbus. He had promised to take his daughter, Danielle. I'd told him to go; I didn't want to ruin their plans. Cheryl stayed with me in the hospital. I called and told him the doctor wanted to deliver Taylor the next day. However, Roger and I were very together on our decisions about Taylor.

I hung up the phone and told the doctor, "We set the date of June 9th, and that's what we would like to stick with."

He said, "Okay, I will dismiss you and we will see you in two weeks."

No one could figure out what had caused me to be so ill, except perhaps the painting I'd done the day before, plus all the trips up and down the ladder. The next day Roger came and picked up Cheryl and me. Since I had an appointment scheduled with Dr. Winters that day, we stopped at the clinic in Defiance on our way home.

Dr. Winters was surprised to see us and asked, "What are you doing here? Dr. Wood said you were delivering today."

We explained our decision to him. To this day I wonder if he thought we were doing the right thing. God is the only one who knows if it was right or wrong, but we felt in our hearts we had made the best decision.

† Chapter 4 †

June 2005

June 9th finally arrived and it was time to go to the hospital! Roger and I left early. My daughter Michelle and her boyfriend Gary were going to be at the hospital for the big day. Also planning on coming were my cousins Rhonda and Cheryl, with whom I am very close. I was filled with a mix of emotions—excited, yet at the same time, scared.

Everything was so uncertain.

Before we left, our pastor came to pray with us. He lifted up the baby in prayer and the doctors and nurses who would be taking care of her.

After we got to the hospital, surgery was pushed back because of an emergency case. Then it was pushed back again. Instead of 9:00 a.m., it was 1:00 in the afternoon before Dr. Wood came in. He explained that there would be several people coming in to talk to us before surgery. We already knew Dr. Wood planned on delivering Taylor by C-section, to cut down on stress to the baby and in anticipation of the complications they were expecting.

The head neonatologist came in and began asking questions. It was going fine until she asked, "Do you want us to revive her when she's born?"

Already tense and on edge from all the waiting, I shouted, "How do you know you'll have to?"

"Oh," she said, "we always have to with these kids."

Roger and I didn't hesitate and at the same time said, "Yes. Do it."

The doctor wrote Revive on Taylor's chart and left the room.

A nurse came in right before we headed for the operating room and said, "We can't find the test results from the amniocentesis. Did you have it done at this hospital?"

My immediate thought was maybe it had all been a big mistake. But, no, it was real. The clinic in Defiance was contacted and Dr. Winters had the results faxed back to Toledo. They never did find the original results of the amniocentesis.

At this point, everything was ready. Roger was in his scrubs, ready for the operating room. Michelle teased him, as she always has, and told him how professional he looked. She kept calling him Dr. Tumblin. We laughed—something we all needed.

I went into the OR first and numbing medicine for the spinal was administered.

I told the nurse I could still feel my feet, to which she replied, "You just think you can."

Just then Dr. Wood came in with his hands in the air as he waited for sterile gloves. He said, "Are we ready?"

I jerked the sheet off my feet, and moving them back and forth as fast as I could, said, "Look! I can still feel my feet!"

The nurse quickly said, "No, Dr. Wood, we're not ready." She repeatedly said to me, "I'm so glad you did that."

"*I'm* so glad I did that!" I told her.

After that, Roger was brought in to sit up by my head, on my left side. There were around 35 people in the room to take care of us. Eventually they began and when I felt the familiar tugging and pulling I remembered from my first C-section. I turned to Roger and said, "What was I thinking? I am too old for this."

It wasn't long before Dr. Wood said, "Here she is! She's out!"

It was 1:17 p.m., June 9, 2005.

We didn't see Taylor at all because she was immediately taken to the next room. We could see the crowd of nurses and doctors, but not Taylor.

Tears ran down my face as I told Roger, "She's not crying. That's not good."

Always good at trying to make me feel better, he said reassuringly, "Maybe she cries very quietly."

Finally they came back, pushing Taylor in a covered Isolette, on their way to the neonatal intensive care unit (NICU).

Roger asked, "Can Kelly see her for a second?"

The nurse stopped and held up our baby's little head and we got a glimpse of her. It was so brief, I really didn't see her. All I knew was she was alive and breathing.

In recovery, I was wide awake and everyone was allowed in to visit with me. Roger, Michelle, Gary, Rhonda, and Cheryl were all there. The time dragged as we waited forever for news.

Michelle had us cracking up because she would poke my leg and ask, "Can you feel that?" She kept poking me and asking, "Well, do you feel that?" The laughter helped to bring the stress level down.

Hours passed and we had not heard a word. Every time we asked, the nurses would tell us that they hadn't heard anything yet. Michelle was getting impatient. After about four and a half hours, Roger asked a nurse if they could just let Michelle see her because they needed to head back home, about a two-hour drive.

Finally, a nurse came in and took Roger and Michelle to see Taylor. Michelle took some photos of her baby sister with a disposable camera.

She came back and told me, "She's so cute! She has dark hair. She's on oxygen, but not a lot."

Roger said, "Kelly, she's okay! She doesn't have Trisomy 18!"

I asked, "How do you know?"

"She looks completely normal. She's just very small," he said.

Rhonda, Cheryl, and I were desperately hoping this was true. Finally, about five hours after Taylor was born, they wheeled me to the NICU and rolled my bed up next to hers.

I knew what to look for.

When I said, "Roger, she does have Trisomy 18," he just looked at me. "She has the clenched hands and her little finger is almost as long as the rest. That little finger kind of wraps around the outside of the rest of them," I explained.

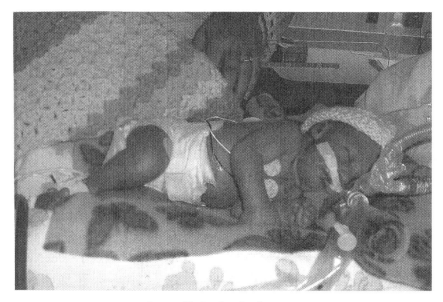

Seeing Taylor for the first time

They were traits listed in the research I had done. A very nice nurse, Pauline, had been called in to take care of Taylor. She told us that the doctors would come and talk to us after I was settled in my room.

Dr. Wood came in and said, "She is doing remarkably well. She is on a little oxygen. She weighs four pounds, four ounces and is very small. We hope she will be able to eat from a bottle, but it will be a couple days before we know that." He continued, "She will need surgery tomorrow because she has an umbilical hernia that will need fixed right away."

The type of hernia Taylor had was called an omphalocele—a birth defect that causes some of the baby's bowel to protrude through an opening in the belly. The exposed bowel was covered with a thin membrane, but surgery needed to be done right away.

"She also has a heart defect," he continued, "but a cardiologist will be in to talk to you about that. A genetics doctor will be in as soon as he is done checking Taylor out."

After everyone left I needed a breather. Even though I'd just had surgery that afternoon, we walked down to the NICU several times.

Nineteen years earlier, when I had my first C-section for my son Mitch, I didn't handle it very well. It took me two days to get moving. But after Taylor was born, no matter how much it hurt, I had to get down to the NICU and see her. I was a lot older and tougher. With great effort and a few groans, I made it.

The cardiologist, Dr. Smith, consulted with us next. He stood at the foot of my bed and said, "I will be Taylor's heart doctor, but there are some things you should know about what I expect. All I ask is that my parents know their child's condition and diagnosis."

He explained the reason he wanted us to be knowledgeable. If Taylor was rushed to the hospital we needed to know what to tell them because in an emergency there isn't time to figure things out. He stood firm as he quizzed us as to when we would go for appointments. He also instructed us to carry cards listing Taylor's diagnosis, her heart condition, and what to do and not to do for her. We were to have those cards with us at all times. Later, I would appreciate this because the information saved her life at least twice.

However, those experiences were still in our future.

We waited for the genetics doctor. When he arrived, he confirmed Taylor had Full Trisomy 18. He told us she was doing well, that there was nothing we could've done to prevent it, and that it was not inherited.

He then shared, "We have another baby with Trisomy 18 in the NICU right now, but he is not going to make it." He was right; that baby passed away at twelve days old. Through all of this, I kept wondering, *What makes me think mine will make it?*

The surgery to repair Taylor's umbilical hernia was performed that same evening. Because of the omphalocele, she didn't develop a belly button, but the surgeon did a great job in creating one. With that first surgery, the first step was taken. Next we had to wait for her intestines to start working.

Dr. Wood came in and reported, "Taylor's Apgar scores were good."

I had never heard of Apgar scores before then. They are numbered scores babies receive at birth based on their muscle tone, pulse, respiration, skin color, and reflexes. Apgar scores are measured at one and five minutes after the baby is born. Despite all her problems, Taylor scored seven and 10, which were good. She didn't cry spontaneously at birth, which is why we didn't hear her.

Dr. Wood said we would have to pray and wait.

Roger's daughter, Danielle, came up to see Taylor that evening. The only thing she said to me was, "She is so tiny. I never saw a baby that small."

Newborn Taylor in the NICU

† CHAPTER 5 †

June 2005

Taylor was the prettiest baby. Of course, I was always partial because I'm her mom. She had very dark brown hair and dark brown eyes. And she was so tiny. She also had a skin tag on her right eye that connected the top and bottom lids, preventing her from opening it. She looked like she was winking at us all of the time. It would be fixed at a later date because it wasn't hurting her, and she had so many other issues that needed attention first.

Taylor had a lot of visitors while she was in the NICU. This was allowed because it wasn't respiratory syncytial virus (RSV) season yet. When RSV and flu season arrived, it would be a different story.

People were fascinated by our daughter. She was holding her own, yet I knew God had His hands on her. Without Him and prayer she wouldn't have been there. She was on supplemental oxygen for less than 24 hours. A feeding tube was inserted into her nose and from there it ran down her throat and into her stomach. Amazingly, she could take a bottle, but wasn't eating enough to meet her nutritional needs. Everything I could do for her, they let me do—and I tried to do everything.

When assigned to Taylor for the day, hospital staff members would say, "All right! I have Taylor today." It also meant an easier day for them, because I wanted to do it all. I knew I needed to learn all I could so I would be prepared when it was time to take her home.

For the first few days after she was born, Taylor was secluded in a room by herself. Although she had tubes running everywhere, she was

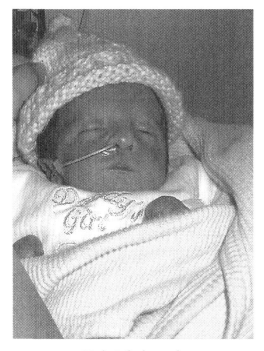

Taylor's feeding tube

doing well. Pauline, the nurse who had been so kind to us from the beginning, came in the third morning after Taylor was born.

"When will Kelly get to hold her?" Roger asked her.

"No one has gotten her out of her bed yet?"

"No," he said. "I didn't want to ask because of all the equipment."

She said, "We will let her hold Taylor right now."

Pauline handed Taylor to me. What a feeling to hold our little daughter for the first time! I will never forget it. The baby they said we would never hold was alive. Alive and beautiful. Then Roger held her. We took a lot of photos. I fed her a bottle, then tube fed her. I was scared and excited at the same time.

Taylor was moved out onto the main NICU floor where there were about twenty babies. Some weighed one pound, some two pounds. I was amazed at what they can do for premature babies and babies with serious complications.

A woman from human services came in to talk to me about Taylor's care when she got home. She asked, "What county do you live in? We will need to get a doctor lined up. She won't be able to leave the hospital without one."

I told her the name of our clinic.

Then she said, "We will need to call in Hospice."

"Why?" I asked.

"You won't be able to take care of her yourself."

That is not at all what we wanted for our daughter.

"Why can't we have visiting nurses come in?" I asked. "We don't need Hospice, nor do we want them."

This began the search for Taylor's home healthcare. A nurse came in with the great news that they'd found a pediatrician at our clinic willing to accept Taylor as a patient and had arranged for visiting nurses to come to our home three days a week. The next step was to order a specially made car seat from March of Dimes, so that she could lie down and still ride safely in the car.

Taylor already had her own car seat and I asked if we could at least try it first. The nurse agreed to a test fit, saying she couldn't make any promises. That's all I wanted—just the opportunity to try. The requirement was that Taylor had to be able to sit upright in the seat for at least 45 minutes without experiencing any breathing difficulties.

When I called Roger later, I told him to bring Taylor's seat when he came up. Taylor had passed her car seat test with flying colors!

The day when photos were taken, the nurse in charge of Taylor was so nice. Rhonda had bought her a darling preemie outfit. . .all purple and white. It was so tiny, yet it was still too big. It didn't matter, though—Taylor was adorable. Because of the problem with her eye, she was winking in her picture. That photo will always be one of my favorites.

Now Taylor was ready to move to another part of the NICU where there were about 15 babies. Although I was ready to be released, she wasn't. Dr. Wood, the OB who had helped deliver her, came in to sign

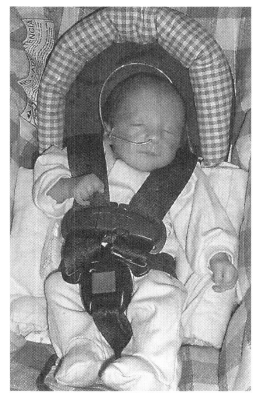

Taylor in her own car seat

my release papers. We talked for a long time. I told him how much we appreciated him and what he had done for Taylor, Roger, and me.

I must have had a big smile on my face, because he said, "Kelly, you act like she's going to go to kindergarten. She's not."

"How do you know?" I asked.

He simply replied, "These kids never live that long."

As he was leaving the room, I said to him, "Dr. Wood, I will send you a kindergarten picture in five years."

He said, "You do that. I'll be expecting it in the mail."

"You'll get one, don't worry!"

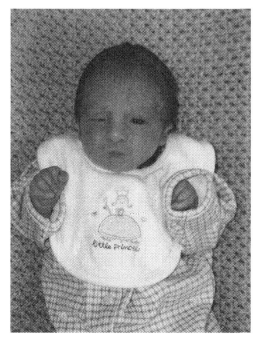

Picture day!

CHAPTER 6

June 2005

Although I had been released from the hospital, Taylor was still a patient. Fortunately, I was able to stay nearby in a building behind the hospital that used to be a dorm for nursing students. It had been remodeled into a place to stay for patients' parents. They had everything we could possibly need, including a washer, dryer, and fridge. Plus, it was a lot cheaper than a hotel.

It was handy because I needed a breast pump. I didn't breast-feed my other kids, but with Taylor I knew it was crucial. So I pumped the milk, put it in the fridge to take to hospital for Taylor the next day. I continued this for about nine weeks. They thought Taylor would never make it that far. But, a lot of things they expected didn't apply to her. When they began discussing sending her home she weighed three pounds and 10 ounces.

"I thought babies had to weigh five pounds before they could go home?" I asked one of the nurses.

She was so kind when she told me, "They figure you should take her home and enjoy what time you have left with her. There's really nothing else we can do for her here. You need to learn how to put her feeding tube in and take it out, and then she can go home."

I said, "Let's get started!"

And we did. The nurse put that tube right down and pulled it right out. Down again and out. I was a nervous wreck—scared to death.

She said, "It's not as hard as you think."

It was my turn next. The nurse made it look so easy. But it wasn't. It didn't go right down. I was crying. Taylor was crying.

"Just focus on putting it into the center of her face," she said.

I did and it slipped right in! WOW! I did it! From that point on I practiced and practiced. Taylor was so calm, although I'm sure she was thinking, *I hope Mom gets this soon.* Taylor was a tough kid.

Since I had gotten the hang of inserting Taylor's feeding tube, the nurse was going to talk to the doctor. It was possible the next day we would be going home. After speaking with the nurse, Dr. Sean from NICU came in.

He said, "Kelly, we can't make any promises, but she is ready to go home. We are thinking she might have thirty days to live. We can't be sure."

I told him, "We will do our best to take care of her and we'll have to see what happens."

The next day I was excited and scared at the same time. We had taken CPR classes, but now that we were face to face with "it's all in your hands now," it was a completely different story.

The day did not get off to a good start. Early in the morning I was packing Taylor's things.

Out of the blue, the nurse assigned to Taylor for that shift said, "You don't have a clue, do you?"

I said, "Excuse me?"

She said, "She isn't going to live. She has Full Trisomy 18. They don't live. You must not get that."

I said, "No, I get that. They also said she wouldn't be born alive and here she is."

She said, "Dr. Smith is going to send her home with oxygen and that isn't going to save her either. This is a death situation. There's no getting around that."

I told her, "I have researched this for months. I know what to expect and I think you should stick to nursing and not giving your opinion."

I didn't talk to her the rest of the day. It wasn't worth it. She was a know-it-all. Whenever she asked me anything or tried to talk to me,

I didn't answer. I will never forget her name and I still harbor dislike toward her. She shouldn't have been in nursing with that attitude. It's one thing to face reality; it's another to steal someone's hope.

Dr. Smith, the cardiologist came into the room. He informed us an appointment for Taylor was scheduled in one month at his Toledo office and that he would most likely see her on a monthly basis.

When he said, "She isn't going home on oxygen," I resisted the impulse to ask him if he thought he should consult Taylor's nurse first. When Taylor was released from the hospital later that day, she weighed just three pounds and 13 ounces. It was unusual for a baby weighing so little to go home, but we were going to try our best and see if our little fighter would stay strong.

Roger came to get us. He loaded the car and took care of my room because there was no way I would leave Taylor by herself with that nurse.

Finally it was time to buckle our baby girl into her car seat. She was so tiny her head only came halfway to the top. I was glad a nurse we really liked walked us outside. She carried Taylor in her car seat down to the car. The seat locked onto a base on the backseat and faced backward. I sat on the seat beside Taylor. At last, everyone was buckled in and we were ready to go. It turned out to be a wonderful day!

About halfway on our two-hour trip home, paranoia kicked in. The questions came fast, furious, and frightening.

What if her heart stops? Will I be able to help her?

What is going to happen to her? Dr. Sean said maybe 30 days.

Would it be today or tomorrow?

It was all too overwhelming and absolutely terrifying.

But, if she could fight and be strong, then so could I!

Those 30 days ended up being the longest I have ever lived through.

We arrived home and I started setting things up so she would always be close to us. The bassinet was placed in the living room. My brother and sister-in-law, Tim and Janet, had sent a monitor for her that had a TV screen on it. We put it in the top of the bassinet and aimed it right down on her so I could see and hear her at all times. It was a big help.

My wonderful cousin Cheryl was at the house with her girls. From the monitor we could hear Hailey and Sydney's conversation about how cute Taylor was and how small she was.

I yelled from the kitchen, "I can hear everything you're saying and I can see you, so don't be playing with her toys."

They laughed.

The first night home, I put the bassinet at the end of our bed. That was the last time for that! We moved her right beside our bed. Her cry was like a baby kitten. Although it was so soft that we could barely hear her, I always did. As a result, I got very little sleep, but she was worth missing out on some sleep. She wasn't hooked up to an apnea machine. I was always thinking, *Thirty days. Thirty days. . .*

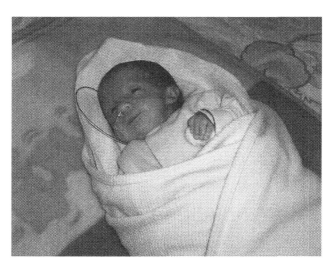

Taylor at home with her Care Bears

27

† Chapter 7 †

June 2005

Worrying became a member of the family. We were always on alert, always waiting for something to happen. We didn't know what it would be. It felt as if we were always on the verge of something happening. We could never relax and were constantly on edge. And the entire time, I kept thinking, *Thirty days. Thirty days. . .*

Taking care of Taylor required a completely different set of rules than for a typical healthy baby. She couldn't have a normal bath as she had to be mostly covered at all times. She couldn't get chilled because it could lead to a cold or pneumonia. So I had to be very careful and fast with her diaper changes and daily hygiene. She wore a hat for a

At home with Taylor

long time, sometimes every day and all day. Her temperature had to be checked hourly to make sure it wasn't too low. We had to be very careful that visitors didn't have colds or coughs, or had been around anyone who did.

Taylor didn't eat very well, but I kept telling myself it was because she was so small. She was able to drink some out of a bottle, and then the rest was put down the feeding tube at the rate of one ounce every three hours. It took around two hours to get it all down and then it was almost time to start all over again.

Taylor began having crying fits at night after Roger left for work. He worked nights and every night about 11:00 p.m. Taylor began to cry. Up to this point, she had not been a crier at all, so this was very out of the ordinary. It wasn't her regular crying. . .I knew something was wrong, but had no idea what. It went on for about a week and a half. I began to wonder if she had acid reflux, so I called Dr. Thread. He checked her over and put her on Prevacid. After two days, the crying stopped. We also kept her sitting up at a 45-degree angle. That, plus the medicine, seemed to do the trick.

Visiting nurses were scheduled to come in three days a week, Mondays, Wednesdays, and Fridays. I'll never forget the first visit.

The nurse came in and she looked at Taylor and said, "Is this Taylor?" I said, "Yes."

"She is not what I was expecting," she said. "She looks good; she's just very small."

Every time the nurses came, they listened to Taylor's heart, checked her pulse, and weighed her. They checked the usual stuff to chart how she was doing. Weight gain was very slow. Taylor was the only baby I ever knew that actually got good, long use out of preemie clothes.

Most people understood how important it was to be clean and not visit if they were sick. On the few occasions someone who had a cough came to visit, I felt so bad to have to ask them not to hold Taylor. I learned very early that the germs can be viable five days before you know you have something and five days after you think it's gone.

We had such great support from our family and friends. Their love and generosity were amazing. Roger, our kids, and my brothers and sisters-in-law were so good even though they lived at a distance. My brother Tim and his wife Janet were in Alaska. My brother Mike and his wife Stacy and their kids had been transferred through his job to Alabama. If our families could help with anything, all we had to do was ask.

Taylor may have been small, but she had a huge bunch of supporters. She received an unbelievable number of all kinds of gifts: clothes, toys, and stuffed animals. Her room was so full it had to be very organized in order to find anything.

Everyone was intrigued by her. She was a baby who wasn't supposed to be with us for one day. I think people wanted to see our miracle sent to us by God.

My Uncle Randy came to see her the first time.

"Would you like to hold her?" I asked.

"No, I'm afraid I will break her," he said.

"I've been taking care of her and if I haven't broken her, nobody can!" I said.

He finally agreed and held her so gently and still. After some time he said, "You better take her back."

After that, Uncle Randy was one of Taylor's biggest fans. I could always count on him to check in and see how we were at least once a week.

My cousin, Gene, rode a bike for exercise. We live across town from him. He often cycled over to stop in and see how she was doing. This really meant a lot to us. I hope they know that. I never needed to call them; they came on their own.

The day of our first appointment with Dr. Thread, the pediatrician, arrived. He gave her a thorough checkup.

He said, "She looks good, but you can see the Trisomy 18 traits: short sternum, low set ears, rocker-bottom feet, little head, small mouth, her clenched hands, and the roof of her mouth is very high. But all in all, she looks very good."

He was very patient with me and answered every question. We made her next appointment for two weeks later.

We took Taylor for her one-month visit with Dr. Smith, the cardiologist, in Toledo. At that point, she weighed about five pounds and was still wearing preemie clothes. He had the nurse do an echocardiogram.

When he got the results he told us, "She's got a lot going on, but I think we will wait until she's three months old and then we'll see about her heart surgery. I will see her next month. She really needs to have some weight on her. So we'll try to buy her some time."

Taylor had a big hole in the center of her heart. It affected all four chambers, but Dr. Smith said she seemed to deal with it very well.

Thirty days passed.

The visiting nurses were still coming to the house and were shocked and surprised Taylor was still on their list of patients. She wasn't supposed to have lived. She wasn't growing, in fact, in many ways she still

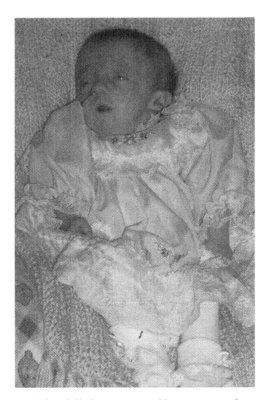

Taylor dolled up in one of her many outfits

seemed like a newborn. But even though she was still tiny, she continued to do well on her own and was reaching some milestones of infancy. She smiled at us and that was worth a million bucks. She frowned at us. . .and *that* was worth a million bucks!

With each passing day, she amazed us. Always in the back of our minds, though, we wondered how long it would last. The thirty days were gone. Now what? Did the stress we felt let up? No, absolutely not! I was constantly on edge and paranoid about every little thing.

† Chapter 8 †

August 2005

Taylor began to coo just like a normal baby. I would say, "What are you yelling about, Taylor?" In response, she "talked" back like she was answering me. She made eye contact and tracked things very well. She wasn't able to hold things. She would be well into her therapy before she was able to grasp or reach for objects. Her hands were always in fists. A nurse in the NICU taught us to roll up little pieces of gauze and put them in her palms because her hands were so tightly clenched. She also wore Velcro splints.

I wanted to take good care of Taylor and tried to keep a close eye on every detail so any symptom, anything unusual would not be overlooked. I knew it would be better if things were attended to early rather than later. I noticed that sometimes she experienced jerking of her face and arms. I videotaped the strange movements and called Dr. Thread's office. They got her in right away. After viewing the video I'd taken, he suggested we take Taylor to a neurologist.

The neurologist we were sent to couldn't have been more cold and unfeeling. He said, with her chromosome defect, he couldn't figure out why Taylor was still here. He ordered some tests. When we went back for the results, his finding was that her brain was far behind other babies her age. We expected that.

Then he said, "Let me hold her." He held her straight up in front of him, and looking her in the eyes, said, "She will never socially smile, never track things, and never coo." As he handed her back to me, he asked, "Why did you do this? She will be a vegetable all her life."

I knew what he meant. *"Why did you have this baby? Why do you want her to live this way?"*

I replied, "She *can* smile; she *can* track things; and she *can* coo. This fighting is *her*, not us."

We stepped outside his office and we could hear as he recorded the session on his machine: *"Mother* says she can smile. *Mother* says she can track things and *mother* says she can coo."

I looked at Roger and said, "We better get out of here before I punch him."

We left, but his office staff kept calling to schedule the next appointment. I wouldn't schedule one. Finally, I told the person on the phone that I didn't like his manner when he talked to us and that I wouldn't be rescheduling. That was the last we heard from that doctor's office.

My brother, Mike, told me all along, "You don't need negative doctors. There are plenty out there. Find another one."

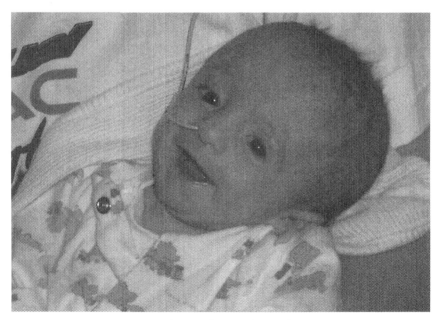

Taylor's million dollar smile

We did find another doctor and he was great. However, when in his waiting room, we experienced just how cruel and unfeeling people can be. We waited for almost three hours. Fortunately, we had the television to entertain us and help pass the time. Two women came in with a little boy and sat down. We didn't pay much attention to them at first until I became aware that they were looking at Taylor and whispering back and forth, sometimes even going so far as to point at her. I assumed they were talking about the feeding tube in her nose. But they just didn't stop! By then I was angry. I couldn't believe how rude they were. We knew we had to deal with people's reactions to Taylor, but these women were old enough to know better. Although I was seething, I ignored them, not an easy task for me, and kept playing with Taylor.

About an hour later, a woman entered the waiting area with a baby girl in a stroller. The little girl had a tracheotomy and coughed a lot. Her mom had to clean out the trach frequently with a portable suction machine. Well, that really got those other two going. They pointed and whispered and even giggled sometimes. That did it. I was furious.

"You two are the rudest people I have ever seen!" I shouted.

They stared at me and one of them said, "What are you talking about?"

I said, "I can't believe two grown women can sit and talk about two babies the way you two have. I was mad enough about the way you kept pointing at my daughter, but the second baby comes in and you just keep it up! My mom always told me if you don't have something nice to say, say nothing! That's what you two should do: *Say nothing!*"

About that time the receptionist stepped out to the waiting room and asked if everything was okay.

I said, "I'm okay, but these two have a problem."

She just walked back into the office. I continued to give the two women the evil eye until I calmed down.

There will always be people who act that way. You have to turn the other cheek or stand up and say something.

I had never said anything before, but I was on overload that day. I stood up and said something.

❀ ❀ ❀

It was time to fix the tag preventing Taylor from opening her right eye. It was left alone at birth. A few weeks later she was to go to Toledo to have it repaired. The eye doctor was very nice. Because Taylor had to be very still, someone would have to hold her during the procedure. I knew I couldn't do it, so Roger did. She screamed. I cried and couldn't watch.

As soon as she was done, I picked her up, hugged and kissed her, and told her that I was so sorry. Suddenly, through my tears, I saw an even more beautiful baby. It was the first time I had seen her with both eyes wide open.

I exclaimed to Roger, "She's even prettier than before!"

A few weeks later Taylor had another appointment with the eye doctor to have her eyes checked.

"Her sight is great!" he said. "Maybe she can see better than either of us!"

Such good news! We didn't know if her eyes would be okay or not. Taylor was a very determined little girl and so far she had passed with flying colors. She was proving all the statistics wrong.

❀ ❀ ❀

By the time Taylor was born, I'd already had many losses in my life and endured much grief and sadness. My mom passed away from ALS—amyotrophic lateral sclerosis (Lou Gehrig's disease)—in 1990. In 2002, my sister Kathy died of cancer at the age of 42. Two years later Roger's dad also died of cancer.

With my pregnancy, my relationship with my maternal grandmother had become very strained. She was upset with me because I was pregnant and Roger and I were not married. Although we planned on getting married, she refused to talk to me for a long time. It made things so much harder with Mom and my sister gone. Now I didn't have my grandmother to talk to, either. However, once we knew the Trisomy 18 diagnosis, I'd made the decision that the baby was the one who needed my energy, care, and concern at that moment.

After Taylor was born, I heard through the grapevine that Grandma was calling people to tell them about the baby. The first week of July, I called my cousin Cheryl.

"Will you go to Grandma's with me so she can see Taylor?" I asked.

She said, "Yes, I called Grandma and she told us to come on out."

When Cheryl, Taylor, and I arrived at Grandma's, she couldn't take her eyes off her tiny great-granddaughter. I gave Taylor to my 91-year-old grandma to hold and that's all it took.

She kept saying over and over, "She's beautiful and so small. . .just like a doll baby. . .maybe even smaller."

She cradled Taylor in her arms for so long, I worried she would become worn out. I kept asking, "Are you tired of holding her?"

"No," Grandma answered.

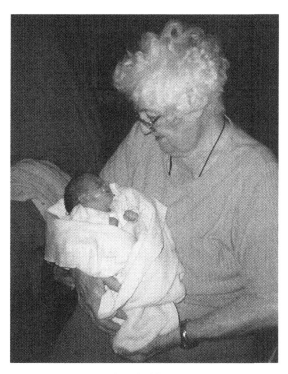

Grandma holding Taylor

After our visit, Grandma called every day. She wasn't interested in how I was; she wanted to check on the baby! A couple weeks later, Grandma was admitted to the hospital and died shortly after. I still miss her and am so thankful things were patched up between us before she passed away.

We rarely took Taylor out for fear she might catch something from all the germs floating around. While the family was going through my grandma's things in preparation for an estate sale, my daughter Michelle came over to stay with Taylor so we could keep her at home. When the day of the sale came, I took Taylor along. I settled her in her stroller and kept her all covered up. My Uncle Pud (Ralph) came to take my place at the sale early, so I could take Taylor back home.

Shortly after the sale, when Taylor was about six weeks old, she was admitted to the hospital. It was July 30th, and the first time she had been back in since she was born. She had not really been ill, but she just wasn't acting like her normal self either. She was whiny and didn't have her usual energy. It was frightening. . .she couldn't tell us in words how she was feeling.

Because of her size, it was an ongoing problem to get enough fluids into her and she had become dehydrated. While we were in the hospital, Dr. Smith, the cardiologist, warned us about contact with other patients and visitors.

"Don't let anyone in her room from neighboring rooms," he said. "That's the fastest way to get her sick." He always said, "Hospitals are germ pools and she could pick up anything here."

The nurses were trying to get an IV catheter inserted and weren't having any success. It was the first of many, many attempts because Taylor's tiny veins had a tendency to roll out of the way of the needle. It was like a contest for some staff members, determined to be the one to accomplish it. Over the next four years, this attitude would often cause me to lose my temper.

That day the IV finally ended up being inserted into Taylor's scalp. A spot had to be shaved on her head to make a place for it. Thank goodness she was taken to a procedure room while it was done so I didn't have to watch. It just tore me up to have to see her go through anything painful. When the staff brought her back, she had a perfect bald square on the left side of her head. I was given a piece of paper with hair taped on it. Written on it were the words: TAYLOR BROOKE'S FIRST HAIR CUT. It was a thoughtful gesture and I was so glad they did that.

"You better not take up hair cutting on the side," I said. "You guys stink at it."

We all laughed.

While we were there, I would just sit and look at Taylor in the hospital crib and think, *Will she have to spend most of her life in hospitals?* But our little girl was a fighter. The more she experienced, the tougher she got. After three days, she was doing well, and we were allowed to take her home. That first admission was my first lesson in prevention. Now I knew what to watch for so I could catch the symptoms a lot earlier. As for preventing dehydration, we would have to push her into drinking as much as she could handle. It was at this time Dr. Smith put her on the medication digoxin to help regulate her heart rate.

It had turned to August while Taylor was hospitalized. She was almost two months old. Roger and I had planned on being married by that time, but with Taylor's health problems we decided to wait. We wanted to have a hog roast for our wedding reception and although we hadn't had the wedding yet, we went ahead with plans for a big family get-together and hog roast.

My brother Tim and his wife, Janet, came from their home in Alaska to visit that week. I was so glad they were able to be there, because they were able to meet Taylor and spend some special time with her. And Janet was such a great help with the party. August 18, 2005, the day of the hog roast, was a big day for us. Our family and friends all came to celebrate with us, enjoy each other and the great food. Although it was August, Taylor was still very small so we kept her snuggly wrapped the entire day. Only a few people held her. However my cousins, Cheryl and Rhonda, were comfortable with her and held her a lot.

I can't think of anything better than time spent with family and friends. After what we had been through since receiving Taylor's diagnosis, we needed to share some fun and laughter.

† CHAPTER 9 †

September 2005

W e took Taylor back to see Dr. Smith, the pediatric cardiologist, for a checkup. He listened to Taylor's heart and reported to us.

"No change," he said. "This is good, because we really need her to gain some weight before heart surgery. So, we will go to the six-month-old time frame and see what happens."

Dr. Smith outlined Taylor's care plan for us. We were to continue seeing him on a monthly basis. I was relieved because I could tell he cared about her and wanted to see her progress. This doctor was one we needed. Before we left that day, Dr. Smith said something to me that would change my outlook.

He said, "Kelly, you are wasting precious time."

"What do you mean?"

"You are so worried about Taylor dying, you are not enjoying her," he said. "We are all going to die and we don't know when. You need to not think about that and just relax and enjoy her."

His advice really changed the way I thought. I still worried and was scared of a lot of things, but I just wanted her to know she how much she was loved. I was letting the worry take all our time—precious time with Taylor that I didn't want to miss.

Taylor decided to ignore medical advice before she came into our world. She had on her best party dress, was having a good time, and was not in a hurry to leave. When, with Dr. Smith's help, we finally realized what we were missing, we followed our daughter's lead and began to enjoy life with Taylor.

She and I started dancing around the kitchen together. We sang songs, and did a lot of other things. Taylor and I didn't watch television during the day. We listened to music all the time, mostly oldies from the early 1960s and 50s.

My cousin Cheryl's daughters, Hailey and Sydney, gave Taylor all their children's books. There were about 50 of them, so Taylor was read a different story almost every day.

Roger doesn't have it in him to make up the character's voices, but Taylor and her daddy had their story time, too. When he read to her, I just cracked up. Sometimes she would fall asleep while he read to her and other times she really looked like she was paying attention. It was so cute because as she got older, sometimes she'd gaze around the room like she was bored with that story and just wasn't into hearing one right then. We learned early that despite her miniature size, Little Miss Taylor had a *big* attitude and we knew what she did and didn't like.

Taylor and I had a nighttime ritual—we called it Taylor and Mom Time. We would lay on our bed together and talk, sing, and laugh. I told her how much we loved her and that we wouldn't have missed her beautiful smile for anything.

Our days continued to be consumed with Taylor's care—starting around 8:00 or 8:30 a.m. and, if all went well, ending around midnight. If she slept at night, it was a bonus and a blessing. We found that her sleeping habits never really improved. Her pediatrician suggested just letting her sleep when she wanted. That wasn't always easy because, long before she wanted sleep, I was often worn out from the daily schedule of feedings, baths, and dispensing her heart medications.

Because she was unable to do it on her own, Taylor required frequent changes of position. If she lay too long in one position, her skin and other tissues might begin to break down and cause sores called decubitus ulcers, also called pressure sores or bedsores. We placed rolled blankets on both sides to keep her in a side-lying position so she wouldn't choke on saliva.

We were told by the doctor that because of the Trisomy 18, Taylor's brain was not able to tell itself to breathe. She could stop breathing and simply not take another breath. As a result, leaving her alone was not in my vocabulary. She was always under surveillance with audio monitors and the video camera monitor my brother and his wife sent us. Taylor's feeding tube caused her to have a little whistle or rattle in her throat when she breathed. Hearing that, I knew she was alive.

I pumped breast milk until she was about nine weeks old and then she was switched to formula. Sometimes her weight would remain the same for weeks—the nurses called it a plateau. The nurses reassured us about her slow and sometimes nonexistent weight gain. "As long as she gains and doesn't lose." Then suddenly she would begin to improve.

Once we had family over and were all playing games and having a good time, when all of a sudden Taylor pulled out her feeding tube. It turned out to be the first of many times she performed that little trick—sometimes up to six or seven times a day she managed to hook her finger into the tubing and jerk it out. That first time turned into quite an event. Despite all the lessons at the hospital, I couldn't get the tube back where it belonged. I was a mess.

After a while, overhearing the ruckus, my brother came into Taylor's room and asked, "Is everything okay?"

Everything wasn't okay. She was crying. I was crying. But finally, it went down. We must have been on stress overload that day.

Things normally went along fairly smoothly, but like for any parent, there were *those* days. If Taylor didn't feel well, she fussed about getting the tube in. If she was fed too fast, the formula came back up. To prevent this from happening, the line had to be shut off for a few minutes and then turned back on. Some days I don't know how she kept it down at all because it seemed like she was fed continuously from the time she woke up until she fell asleep.

August flew by and before long it was September. Here in our little town, Labor Day heralds the big homecoming celebration. It's a weekend crammed with all kinds of fun and festivities for everyone, including rides, parades, games and contests, and food. I didn't attend many of the activities that year because I was so afraid of taking Taylor out around so many people. Plus, it seemed like it was always too hot or too cold or windy or rainy. It just wasn't worth taking a chance. When I did have her up there, people would stop at the stroller to peek in at her. Some were just curious when they asked what the tube in her nose was for. But some people were insensitive, even rude when they asked things like how long she had to live. Many people saw Taylor's beauty and were kind and supportive. They understood she was truly a miracle and offered up prayers on our family's behalf.

My daughter Michelle was around four months pregnant by this time and doing well. When she came over, she held Taylor and they watched TV together. Michelle talked to her little sister and could make her smile about nothing. Taylor just loved Michelle. When Michelle

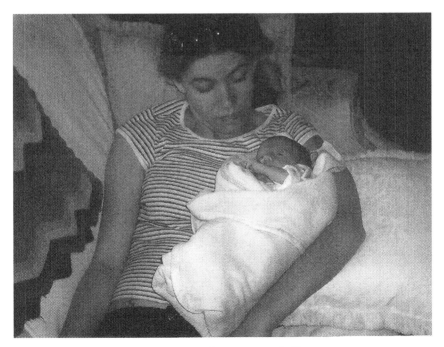

Taylor with big sister Michelle

told me the OB doctor had asked her to take the triple screen blood test, she had said, "No way, I watched my mom cry for months. She couldn't sleep or relax. If she has something, we will find out when she gets here. I knew it was stressful for everyone in the family, but we all knew she was worth it."

A week after homecoming, my cousin Cheryl called and asked Michelle and I to come to her place Saturday night, saying she had picked up some stuff for Michelle's baby. It wasn't just some stuff! Just like with Taylor, she had gone overboard. Cheryl was just as excited about Michelle's baby as we were. There were so many gifts, including a darling bassinet that vibrated and played music. We ended up with so many things, there was barely enough room to get it all into Michelle's car! After we crammed everything into the car, we visited for a while with Cheryl, her two daughters, and one of Cheryl's friends. It started getting late, so we headed home.

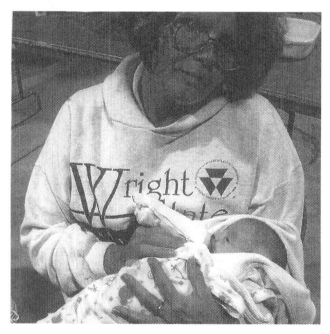

Cheryl with Taylor

Early the next morning the phone rang. It was my Aunt Carolyn, Cheryl's mom. She said they were on the way to the hospital, because Cheryl was being taken there in an EMS squad. Her heart had suddenly stopped. Cheryl passed away at the hospital. She was in her mid-forties.

I thought of her girls, Hailey and Sydney, so young, not even teenagers yet. They had lost their mom. What would they do? Their dad lived in North Carolina. I thought about myself, too. Cheryl was not only my cousin; she had been my lifelong best friend.

Cheryl was the one who, after my sister died and my brothers moved away, said I could be her sister. She and her sisters, my other cousins, had always been so good to me and my family. We were a part of their holidays and cookouts. Whatever their family did, we were included. When it came time to clean out her house, I couldn't help. I tried and I just couldn't. No one expected me to help; they had simply asked if I wanted to. I know it was painful for them too, but I just couldn't do it. Cheryl and I had been close since we were little kids. When I was stressed to the limit, who was I going to call?

My thoughts went back over the past year. She had been Taylor's biggest supporter from the time I found out I was pregnant. I was saddened when I realized Cheryl would miss out on being with Taylor. Yet, I was so glad she was able to spend time with her for three months. She died September 11, 2005, and I still miss her terribly.

CHAPTER 10

October 2005

Taylor began to run low-grade fevers. Michelle, who is a nurse, would kind of laugh when I reported to her that Taylor had a fever.

"What is it?" she'd ask.

It wouldn't be all that high—99.3 or something like that.

"That's not a fever," she said.

But, just like everything else about Taylor, even the smallest deviation from normal meant something could very well be brewing. A low-grade fever often indicated a urinary tract infection. UTIs turned out to be an ongoing problem and Taylor had many during her first three years. As a result, she was prescribed antibiotics far more often than I can count. It didn't get her down, though. Taylor just kept fighting.

Michelle's due date of October 29 was fast approaching. I needed to make plans for Taylor so I could be at the hospital for my first grandchild's birth. I asked my Aunt Mary and Uncle Rog if they thought they could do this for me. Uncle Rog was retired and Aunt Mary didn't work, so timing wouldn't be much of a problem for them. They agreed, but said I needed to tell them about Taylor's care before the big day came. So I made a list and planned on measuring out her meds before she went to stay with them. I took the tiny little bed that Cheryl had given me that had belonged to her girls.

It wasn't long before the day came.

Michelle called and said, "I'm in labor, but Dr. Winters said wait until the contractions are five minutes apart."

The phone calls flew back and forth all day. Michelle only lived two miles away, with Aunt Mary only one mile in the other direction. I packed Taylor's stuff and got everything loaded into the car. Michelle called and said it was time to go. I took off to Aunt Mary's with Taylor. But it was so hard to leave her. Other than hospital stays, it was the only night in her life she spent without me.

After getting Taylor situated, I drove over and picked up Michelle and Gary. We dropped their dog off at Gary's mom's house on our way to the hospital.

"Can't you just run one stop sign?" Michelle kept asking.

I laughed and said, "Safety first!"

When we got to the hospital, Michelle was already dilated to 8 cm.

I told Gary, "Hmm, I bet she's in a lot of pain." We still laugh about that. Well, at least Gary and I do. . .Michelle, not so much!

I called to check on Taylor and asked how she did taking her heart meds. My aunt and uncle reported she was a perfect angel. They don't know how much I appreciated them for watching her. I didn't want to miss Layla's impending arrival.

Layla at six weeks and Taylor at six months

We were going to have two little girls now. I thought about how Taylor and Layla could grow up together and be best friends. When Layla was born at five pounds, 12 ounces, it was the only time they were anywhere close in size and Layla quickly outgrew Taylor.

With everyone doing well, I left the hospital about 7:30 a.m. I knew Aunt Mary probably hadn't gotten much sleep overnight, but I also knew she would have taken excellent care of Taylor.

It was getting close to Christmas. My brother Mike, his wife Stacy, and their kids came from Alabama for the holidays. It was the second time they had seen Taylor and Stacy said she could see a difference in her growth. Even so, Taylor's weight was still under six pounds.

We went to Roger's family Christmas that first year Taylor was here. We didn't stay a long time, but I really wanted his family to see her. She wore a tiny Christmas outfit and looked so cute. We didn't have Christmas for my side of the family since Grandma and Cheryl had died shortly before. We all decided it would be best to wait until the next year to celebrate the holidays together.

Taylor didn't get to go out much. It was cold and I was so afraid she would get sick. Other than going to doctors' appointments, she pretty much stayed home. We went to a scheduled appointment with Dr. Smith, her cardiologist in Toledo. He wanted Taylor to weigh at least twenty pounds before performing surgery, but he was also realistic. He was fairly certain that wouldn't happen. She weighed around seven pounds and was holding her own. We left there with the continuing goal of trying to achieve more weight gain. She was such a tough little cookie!

When we visited Dr. Thread, the pediatrician, for a regular appointment, I told him I was pretty sure her spine was starting to bend. He checked it out, agreed, and had his nurse call Toledo to find an orthopedic doctor to check into it.

The first appointment was with Dr. Brown. He was very young and very nice. After examining Taylor, he agreed her back was bending, but he said we really couldn't do anything until the curvature reached about 70 degrees. They were doctor's terms, and the measurements based on their scale, but what it came down to was that she needed to have a special back brace to prevent the curvature from getting worse.

Next we went to see Don, who ended up making all the braces Taylor needed, including those on her legs. He was such a great guy! We couldn't have gotten a nicer brace guy than Don. We took Taylor to have a mold made of her back so the brace would fit her perfectly.

It didn't take Dr. Brown long to comprehend what a sweet little girl Taylor was. It was obvious from our first encounter with him that he was a doctor who truly cared about his patients.

Every time he came into the exam room, he'd say, "The precious angel is here!"

Taylor wearing her new back brace

He checked out Taylor's brace, made sure everything was right, and told us she needed to wear it 23 hours out of every day. This turned out to be much harder than I thought it would be. The brace was very fitted and snug, reaching from the top of her hips to up under her arms. Because it was lined with a type of foam, it made Taylor very hot and sweaty. She already perspired a lot even before she began wearing her brace.

We discussed the impact of the back brace on the heart surgery with Dr. Brown and he said we could leave it off after surgery because he knew they wouldn't want it squeezing her chest. He was also concerned because she had a flattened area on her head, called a plagiocephaly. Treatment for this condition included a specially made helmet, but I didn't want her going into heart surgery with one. It would be one more thing for her to adjust to, and I thought she already had enough issues to deal with on a daily basis. Her care after heart surgery was going to be daunting without any additional hardware.

Dr. Brown thought it was okay to wait, but was concerned about the time frame because after the age of one, our insurance wouldn't pay for a helmet. We decided to take a chance on that. Besides, I thought, when her hair got longer the flat spot would no longer be visible. We decided to worry about it later unless it began to become an issue. Dr. Brown told us he really didn't expect Taylor to be back to his office because she seemed so weak and small. But she kept returning and seemed to show improvement with every visit.

Along with Taylor's long list of medical conditions, from birth she had serious problems with constipation. It continued to be a concern. We knew if she didn't have a bowel movement every other day, we had better try something. And if that didn't work, it was time to try something else. If things weren't moving, she tended to run a low-grade fever. One night, after I had tried everything I knew without success, we ended up taking her to the emergency room. The medical staff couldn't get Taylor's bowels to move either, so they were preparing to send her to Toledo. Since it was going to be two hours before the squad could pick her up and transport her, Roger requested that we drive her there. We explained it wasn't a life or death situation and we could get her there much faster. As a result, we drove her ourselves. Although we ended up being at the larger hospital overnight, through their efforts—and to our relief, Taylor's bowels finally moved.

While we were there, a doctor noticed Taylor's eyes were crossed. Her eyes had always been that way—one looked straight and the other looked off to the side. The doctor said it wasn't a big deal, but the eyes could be fixed with laser surgery when Taylor got a little older. We had a nice visit with that doctor. She was so interested in Taylor because she hadn't seen a child with Trisomy 18 that had reached Taylor's age.

Although we hardly noticed the difference in her eyes, one time we were at my cousin Rhonda's house and one of my other cousin's kids said, "Isn't that strange, Kelly?"

"What?"

"Taylor's eyes look different ways," he said in all innocence. "How do you know what she's looking at?"

Taylor and Mom

I laughed until I about cried. My cousin, his mom, was so embarrassed. I told her I would rather people ask than talk behind our backs. That's just the way I am. Over time, Taylor's eyes grew stronger and improved without treatment. When we got home from the hospital in Toledo, the visiting nurses came in for another visit. Taylor gained weight at a good rate for the next two months, bringing her weight close to 10 pounds. Each time Taylor gained one pound, we celebrated by ordering pizza on a Friday night. She couldn't eat it, of course, but we always thanked her for gaining the weight so *we* could. Those next couple months were great! We had pizza about every other weekend.

CHAPTER 11

April through June 2006

D r. Smith was off work and on medical leave because he'd had surgery, but he still monitored Taylor from home.

I was sitting at home one night and the phone rang. It was Dr. Smith.

He said, "Kelly, I have been looking at Taylor's last echo [echocardiogram] and I believe it's time to schedule her heart surgery."

He was to get in touch with the hospital at the University of Michigan and let us know the date. Now my nerves were practically jangling. With the exception of Dr. Smith, medical personnel were of a mind that Taylor wouldn't survive the surgery. He said he thought she would get through it.

I was a wreck.

The call came from Michigan. The surgery was scheduled for June 14, 2006. We had to be sure Taylor didn't lose weight. In addition to that, there was so much that needed to be done in preparation.

Mike and Stacy were going to come from Alabama to go with us for the surgery. I had to make arrangements to stay in Michigan for who knows how long. . .One day? Three months? Who knew?

Before we did anything else, though, I asked our pastor about having Taylor dedicated. We set the date for the church service a week before she was scheduled to go into the hospital. Our kids were there, along with Mitchell's girlfriend, plus extended family members. My cousin, Peg, bought Taylor a beautiful dress for that most special occasion. Dressed in it, the sheer pink fabric with satin stripes cascaded to full length, and Taylor looked just like a doll baby.

Both Roger and my churches prayed for our daughter all the time. Many churches, not just locally, but all over the United States, were praying for her. People who didn't even know her or our family were praying for her. I knew we had to turn her over to God.

On June 9th, Taylor celebrated her first birthday. It was such a beautiful day for a party and we had a big one! About 50 people gathered to help us celebrate at a cookout. Guests carried in dishes and we had just about *everything* to eat. And once again, Taylor was inundated with gifts. No one had any idea what the outcome of the surgery would be. Although no one knew if it would be the last time, all our family and friends gathered to see her. We knew it was time for her to have the surgery. She was so sick, pale, and crying. We kept her in the house for most of the party, bringing her out for the cake cutting. We wanted

Dad, Mom and Taylor at her dedication

a photo of her with her cake. She was taken right back in the house after that.

Everyone seemed to have a good time, but I felt so badly that Taylor wasn't feeling well and felt even worse that I didn't know what was wrong with her. We took a lot of pictures that day. I trusted God would do what He thought best, but at the same time I wished He could clue me in ahead of time. I thanked everyone for standing behind us about the decisions we had to make concerning Taylor, and asked them to continue to keep her in their prayers. We knew every birthday was another mountain climbed. It was pure joy to see her hit each milestone that we were told she would never reach.

Mike and Stacy arrived the same day we were to leave for Ann Arbor, Michigan. A woman from the hospital's human services department had reserved a room for us at the Ronald McDonald House (RMH), which was within walking distance of the hospital. Our first day there was spent getting all the pre-op stuff done.

Taylor needed blood drawn, an echocardiogram, and had visits with surgeons and cardiologists. One cardiologist told us we should wait a little longer for the surgery to take place, that there were more medications Taylor could take. Roger, Mike, Stacy, and I discussed it. We talked about what would happen if there was an emergency. We lived so far away and we would have to get her to one hospital, then to another, then to Michigan. What if we didn't have that kind of time?

Then Roger and I said, "Dr. Smith has been taking care of her since the day she was born. If he says it's time for the surgery, then it's time."

We decided to go ahead with the original plans and we did. We spent that entire first day at the hospital. It was evening before we unloaded the cars and truck. With all our gear, it looked like we were moving in permanently, but we were four adults, plus Taylor. I took her bassinet for her to sleep in the first night at the Ronald McDonald House.

I wanted to go out and get supper because we had had such a long day and we were all hungry. So we went out to eat, but Taylor was fussy most of the time. Maybe I hadn't noticed anything was wrong during the day because we were so busy getting here and there, talking to people and everything. But we were all surprised when we got back to the house and there was a message on the machine about Taylor's test results. She needed to be admitted to the hospital that night. So we turned right around and went back out the door.

When we got to the hospital, they explained that Taylor's calcium was at a dangerously high level. Once calcium gets so high, it will start settling in joints and it can be fatal. This is the reason Taylor had been so whiny. She was admitted and her surgery was postponed for a few days. She was hooked up to an IV to get fluids running, which would help get her calcium levels under control. Until those numbers were in a normal range, they couldn't move forward with her surgery.

While Taylor was hooked up to monitors, other problems occurred. Her heart rate usually ran between 145 and 160 beats per minute. Within seconds, it dropped down into the 60s and 70s. They rushed to find the problem, with the conclusion being the meds they

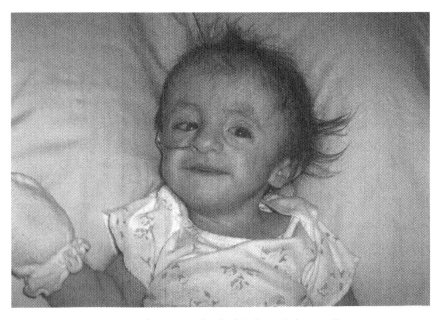

It was obvious Taylor hadn't been feeling well

put her on to lower her calcium were also lowering her potassium, causing heart rate to drop rapidly and without warning.

I stayed with her the first two nights, but as any parent who has ever spent a night in a hospital with a sick child knows, I couldn't rest. There was too much going on all night long. Everyone thought I was getting kind of grouchy. The third night Mike and Stacy stayed through the night with Taylor, so I could sleep at the RMH.

I couldn't have had two better people on the job. The medical personnel were going to start Taylor on oxygen, but Mike stopped them.

"No oxygen," he said. "I have heard Kelly say that for a year."

He told them to call me, but he knew she was not supposed to have any. He was right, and they didn't give her any and she got through it without it. I told him that he did the right thing. If there was one thing I learned over the course of Taylor's life, it was just because someone is a doctor or nurse doesn't mean he or she is always right. This medical staff still didn't know Taylor very well.

Taylor's heart surgery was rescheduled for June 19, 2006. I was so scared. I was nervous and couldn't help wondering if it would be the last time I held her. I cried. Taylor was so small, but it was obvious that the more upset I became, the more she knew something wasn't right. She looked at me like she was scared.

We prayed and prayed.

The surgeon, a very friendly guy with a ponytail, came in and talked to us.

He shook all our hands and said, "Hi, I am Dr. O'Malley. I will be doing Taylor's surgery."

I noticed he had really small hands. I guessed that they would be the best to operate on a tiny baby's heart. He explained how long he thought it would take and what he planned to do and that it would be a waiting game.

When the nurse came in with a wheelchair to take us to the surgical holding area, I asked her, "Do you think Dr. O'Malley slept good last night?"

She laughed and said, "Yes."

"Well, I hope he isn't worried about paying his house payment or car payment."

She laughed and said, "His wife takes care of all that. There is no reason to worry about that stuff. You have enough on your mind. So forget about the small stuff."

We were off to the holding area. I held Taylor while the nurse wheeled us down.

I sat there, hugged Taylor, and kissed her, and prayed and cried. It was the moment that will always top the list of things I hated most. . .handing my daughter over for surgery. I didn't know if she would come out of it or not, and I really didn't know if I could live with that, but I knew I didn't want her to go through it by herself. When I handed her to the staff, it literally broke my heart. I was in pieces. After being told she would never make it through, it was the hardest thing I had gone through so far.

I went to the waiting room and where Roger, Mike, and Stacy were waiting for me. Then the pastor from Roger's church, and the pastor and his wife from my church, came in. We prayed, talked, watched TV, and read some magazines. The tension was like none I had ever experienced. It wasn't long before a nurse came out and told us things were going good. She told us Taylor was hooked up to all the machines and told us she'd come back when there was more news. Her next trip out, she told us that Taylor was still doing well and that the surgeon had her chest open. Those words never left me. I just sat there and imagined her tiny chest wide open. She weighed less than 10 pounds and was a year old. I weighed over 10 pounds when I was born!

I just kept praying for God to please watch over her. Even before she was born, we had known we could lose her at any time, but once she was with us, I just couldn't, and didn't want to, imagine life without her. I was so thankful for the ones who came to be with us. I would've driven Roger crazy, I'm sure, if it had been just us.

The next time the nurse came out, it was to tell us Taylor's heart was patched and although the surgeon was working on something he hadn't planned on fixing, she was doing well.

Finally, the nurse came out and told us that the surgeon was closing and all went well. Taylor did a wonderful job! *Thank You, God!* We all were very happy.

† Chapter 12 †

June 2006

The surgery took about seven hours. Afterward Taylor was taken to recovery. As soon as they got her settled, they let us in to see her. They tried to prepare us, to tell us what to expect before we went in to see her, but, oh my! There were so many IV poles holding all of her medications—sixteen meds total. Tubing ran everywhere. She had the incision on her chest and a ventilator was breathing for her, yet she still looked better than we had expected. Her color was good. She didn't seem very swollen.

There were already concerns being voiced about her ever getting off the ventilator. Would she ever breathe on her own again? We didn't know. They didn't know. It was so scary, seeing all this stuff hooked up to her. Buried under all that equipment in the pediatric intensive care unit, she looked like a little pea, lying in the middle of a twin-sized bed with safety rails.

Her nurse, Mandy, was so nice and we all quickly took a liking to her. We felt reassured that she was going to take excellent care of our daughter. We could stay with Taylor as late as we wanted, but we couldn't sleep there. Mandy told us we could come back whenever we wanted or that we could call as often as we liked. We felt very comfortable with Taylor in Mandy's care. Roger, Mike, Stacy, and I went to the Ronald McDonald House to get some rest.

I called the ICU at about 2:30 a.m. and talked with Mandy, who said, "Taylor just had a bath and I put a bow in her hair. She looks so cute."

I was relieved, slightly. When I called back at 4:00 a.m., Mandy reported, "She's still doing great."

After that call, I finally relaxed enough to fall sleep. We were awakened by the phone at 6:45 a.m. It was the nurse at the nurses' station in ICU. She said, "Is this Kelly? You need to get here as soon as you can."

I asked, "Can you tell me what's going on?"

"All I know is CPR is in progress. Taylor's heart stopped."

"We've got to go!" I said as I hung up the phone. "Taylor's heart stopped and they are doing CPR now."

I can't remember if we even got dressed. Mike ordered Roger and me to go, that they would be right behind us. We drove and parked as fast as we could, and ran upstairs to the unit, but we couldn't go in because they were still working on her. The whole time I was praying, "Please God, stay with her, with Your hands on her. If You have to take her, don't let her suffer." I know we were all praying.

God heard us.

We were in the waiting room forever—at least it felt that way. Mike and Stacy had arrived there shortly after we did. I just kept praying and crying. Finally, someone came and got us. Mandy told us that Taylor had been just fine and resting well, when she suddenly spiked a fever, just that fast. She told another nurse to call Dr. Brian and tell him there was something wrong. When Taylor's temperature shot up to 102 degrees, her heart just stopped. It happened to be shift change and there were a lot of nurses and cardiologists there, so she had many people working on her. If it was going to happen, it couldn't have been at a better time. I thanked the good Lord for that. They'd had to do cardiopulmonary resuscitation (CPR) to get her heart going again. But, even once it had started again, Taylor's heart just couldn't beat fast enough on its own. They'd given her a pacemaker to keep her heat beating at a steady pace.

Roger, Mike, Stacy, and I still believe if Mandy hadn't been taking care of her, Taylor wouldn't have made through that night. We know God has been in charge of all that's happened. He must have thought Taylor's work wasn't finished yet, because she came through. But her fight was just beginning.

She was sedated to keep her from moving around. She needed to be very still to promote healing. Because of Taylor's Trisomy 18 diagnosis, they didn't know what to expect. As a result, everything was carried out with extreme caution. Taylor was still on the ventilator and while it was in her care plan to begin weaning her off, they just didn't know if they would ever be able to take her off of the ventilator, something that had been a serious concern from the start.

She was on 16 different meds at that point and I don't know how they were ever kept straight. Wires from all the monitors were all wrapped up in each other. It looked like Christmas lights when trying to untangle them. We learned at this time that Taylor's liver function wasn't up to par. She began to look puffy and swollen and was becoming jaundiced, causing her skin, eyes, and mucus membranes to take on a yellowish cast. Liver function tests were performed every six hours, with a very close eye kept on the numbers to make sure they headed in the right direction.

After a few liver tests, the numbers appeared to be improving. They continued checking them every six hours and at the same time her potassium level was getting better, too. The ventilator weaning process had been started and Taylor was able to tolerate breathing on her own for a few hours at a time before being put back on the system. Although still not where it should be, her liver seemed to be getting better. But her little body remained swollen and she was very yellow from the jaundice.

Mike and Stacy needed to go get their kids from Stacy's parent's house. My cousin, Diana (everyone calls her Bugg), came and was able to spend some time with Mike and Stacy before they left to go back home to Alabama on June 21st. Diana planned on staying with us that night and the next day.

Roger left when Diana arrived. He was headed back home because he had been hired at a factory shortly before Taylor's surgery date and he needed to report for work. Diana and I were in the ICU with Taylor when the head of the unit came in.

He didn't mince any words when he abruptly said, "Taylor is a very sick little girl. I'm not sure she will make it."

Diana and I just stared at each other as he turned and walked out of the room. I immediately called Roger on his cell phone and repeated what the doctor had said. I was incredibly upset. It really bothered me how he just blurted it out, like he was giving us a weather report.

We were just standing there, trying to absorb this shattering information when Dr. O'Malley came in. He had his hair in a ponytail and was wearing a black suit. I was crying when I told him what the other doctor had just said.

Dr. O'Malley calmly replied, "I expected that. I really believe her liver will start working. I just think it will take time and we can't hurry her."

He reassured me that Taylor was going to be okay; we were going to give her some time.

When he walked out, Diana and I looked at each other, and I asked her, "So, who do we believe?"

She said, "I'm going with the surgeon. He is much more optimistic."

A few minutes later, we were shocked when Roger walked in!

"I thought you were on your way home!" I said.

"I can't leave her when things are so unsure," he said.

He had turned around and come back to the hospital after I called. Through all of this, I felt so bad for our older kids. We were so far away. My son Mitchell called at least once a day. During all this Michelle called at least ten times a day to check on Taylor's condition and to see how Roger and I were doing. With Layla only five months younger than Taylor, plus working, Michelle was exhausted and I didn't want them making the three and a half hour drive to Ann Arbor. During our many telephone calls, Michelle's nurse's training was a big plus as she helped me to understand medical issues, medicines, and so forth as she answered my questions. She suggested issues I might want to bring up and questions to ask the medical staff.

Diana and Roger planned to leave Thursday, June 21st. My Aunt Carolyn, my cousin Rhonda, and Hailey, my cousin Cheryl's daughter, came up that day to spend some time with Diana before she left. They stayed until the 25th. We had been at the University of Michigan Mott Children's Hospital since June 14th. Taylor was still in ICU and had a lot of ongoing issues.

CHAPTER 13

July 2006

Taylor's liver still wasn't working very well and that was affecting her blood's clotting capability. When the line that delivered some of her meds was removed from her chest, bleeding caused blood to build up around one of her lungs, causing her blood pressure to drop. That required the insertion of a drainage tube into her lung. The pacemaker was still in place, and there was no plan for removing it at that time. The doctor felt since it was regulating her heartbeat, why not leave it?

She was resting comfortably at that point and I hoped it would be that way the rest of the night. We went back to the house to get some much needed rest.

Taylor was supported by a lot of people who cared. She received so many cards and so many people called to check on her. Some even made the drive up to visit. We were very blessed.

I talked to Layla, my granddaughter, on the phone whenever I could. When they were older, Taylor and Layla became best buddies. What a pair! Taylor couldn't talk or sit up or even hold her head up, but Layla played with her. Taylor simply sat and watched Layla and laughed at her. It could be 100 degrees outside and Layla would cover Taylor up with blankets and pretend she was taking care of her.

If Taylor moved her legs, Layla told her, "Hold still, Taylor! I'm not done fixing you."

They were so cute together; they made me laugh just watching them. Often, during these times, I wished I could know what Taylor was thinking. I *knew* what Layla was thinking, though. It didn't take her long at all to figure out that when it was time for me to tube feed Taylor, I was busy. And that's when Layla got into things.

Finally Taylor was breathing on her own. The ventilator was turned off during the day. They hooked her back up a few hours during the night. But the medical opinion was that her respirations were slower than they should be. The pacer was still on, but they had started turning down the rate because they wanted her heart to beat on its own. The rate was being decreased very slowly, to allow her a chance to do it by herself. The chest tube was still in place, but the drainage had slowed down a lot. We were hoping and praying this meant she'd soon be stepped down and out of ICU.

The next day, June 25th, Taylor was moved to moderate care, a room where there were five kids cared for by two nurses. However, I stayed there all day. I didn't leave her unless absolutely necessary. After she got there, she cried so hard at intervals she stopped breathing and turned blue. It was incredibly upsetting. Seeing one's child like that is heartbreaking. I asked the nurse what was wrong. She told me Taylor had been sent down without orders for pain meds. Taylor continued to cry for a solid hour and a half, while we waited for pain medicine orders.

The pain was so bad, her apnea machine kept going off. The nurse had to flick the bottoms of her feet to get her to start breathing again.

I was scared to death, but they had to have orders from the doctor before giving her anything. He was in ICU because three kids had coded. Taylor had to wait until he was able to get free and make out an order. Relief arrived for her at last. When she finally got the meds, she immediately went off to sleep—out like a light. Since she was resting well, I went back to the house to get some rest myself. I called two times during the night and was told she was still resting. All the crying had worn her out.

The respiratory therapist visited Taylor and reported that he thought she looked good. Taylor had been out of it for so long, and that came with its own set of problems. She normally slept with her eyes open, but since surgery, she had been sedated which meant her eyes were half-open without blinking for days and a thick crust formed on her eyeballs. They looked awful. Eye drops were started, but it took a couple days to get her eyes back to normal. Because she hadn't been moving at all, she had really stiffened up from lying still for so long. I took some lotion out of her bag and started to massage her legs and arms. By that night she was so much more flexible and those little arms and legs were going to town, swinging and kicking all over. Amen!

In order to start getting some nutrition, a feeding tube was inserted. Before surgery, she usually took about 105 cc every four hours. Now she was started on 52 cc of formula to be given only through the tube. Trying to start bottle feeding would come later.

It was decided to remove the pacer. I prayed that God would please let her be okay without it. The wires attached to her heart were to be left on in case of an emergency. She seemed to do well without it, but was very irritable. I tried to keep her happy, but nothing seemed to be what she wanted. Sometimes she cried and sometimes she laughed.

From birth she had struggled with constipation, but since surgery she had diarrhea all the time, probably from all the antibiotics she was on. She was still receiving an unbelievable 15 or 16 different medications. Mandy, her nurse from ICU, came down to see Taylor, who responded by smiling just like she knew her. I'm sure she did. They had spent a lot of time together in ICU. The nurses came in from the hall to see Taylor smiling so big. I had to take more pictures. Those photos always amazed people who looked at them after we got home. How could she smile like that after what she had been through?

Her next move to the general floor was going to happen soon and there I would be allowed to stay in the room with her. I couldn't wait! Roger came up that weekend and Taylor and I were so excited to see him!

I missed being home with Roger and the kids. I knew Michelle was missing us, and although Mitchell wouldn't come out and say it, we knew he was too. Danielle, Roger's other daughter who lived with her mom and stepfather, called Roger and said she hoped we came home soon. I'm so glad we could all talk to each other whenever we wanted. The next day was my birthday, and while we all felt bad that I wasn't

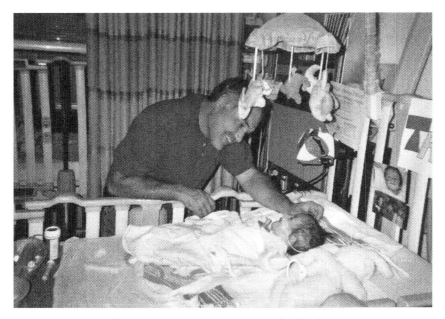

In spite of everything she had been through after heart surgery,
Taylor still had a big smile for her daddy

home, we also knew we could celebrate later. Taylor's well-being was of absolute importance to us all. Roger was so sweet and sent Taylor and I cards, plus a dozen beautiful roses for me. I got lots of calls and birthday cards. I'm so blessed to have such good family and friends.

Rhonda and Buck came to see Taylor. Rhonda held her and actually got her to drink out of her bottle. I'd tried, the nurses had tried, but Rhonda always could get her to do things others couldn't. When Taylor was admitted to the hospital, she drank out of a bottle and had a pacifier. After she was dismissed she refused to ever take a bottle or pacifier again. The nurses teased me because I called her pacifier a "fooler." They said they had never heard it called that and wondered if I called a boy's pacifier a "fool him."

The nurses were so nice and we laughed and joked with them, as they almost became part of our family. They offered to sit with Taylor while I went and did my chores at the RMH. One day while Taylor was

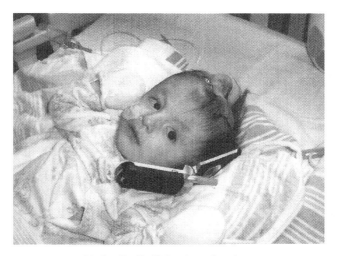

Taylor "callin'" Dad on the phone

sleeping and Roger was home working, I told the nurse I'd just run and do my work real quickly. She told me to take my time. I ran over there, did the chores as fast as I could and came right back. I was walking down the hall and heard Taylor just screaming.

The nurse met me and I asked, "What's wrong with Taylor?"

She said, "She woke up and started crying and I can't get her calmed down. I've tried everything!"

I walked into the doorway of Taylor's room and, as soon as she saw me, she didn't utter another peep.

I said, "Taylor Brooke, you are spoiled."

She was a mommy's girl! I knew she was a true miracle because a doctor said she would never know who we were or what was going on around her.

Roger planned on leaving at the end of the weekend. His niece, Jeannie, and her daughter Kayla, had come to see Taylor that Sunday. Taylor was all smiles for them. It had been a good day, but we still had to contend with less-than-satisfactory lab results. Her magnesium was too low and her blood pressure was too high. Her liver was on the mend and her color was good. Although her mood was so much better, those numbers had to be perfect before she could go home.

The cardiologist came in to check her out. He said they were calling in an endocrinologist to see what he could do help manage the magnesium level. While he was in there, he also said Taylor would just die one day, just stop breathing. The resident, who had gotten close to Taylor, asked him why she wasn't allowed to have an apnea machine.

The cardiologist told him, "Because these kids just die that way."

The resident asked why she couldn't be sent home with the machine if it could prevent that from happening. He persisted and continued to fight for Taylor. It was as if Taylor knew he was on her side. When he came into the room Taylor lit up and smiled the biggest smiles at him. He wore down the powers-that-be with his persistence, because he got the go-ahead to send Taylor home with a monitor. I agreed to take the required CPR classes again and the training it took to learn how to run the machine.

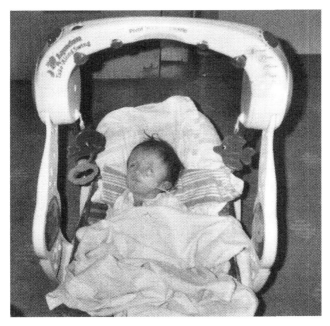

Taylor in the hospital after heart surgery

† CHAPTER 14 †

July 2006

I t was the Fourth of July and we were celebrating our own freedom—
we were actually making preparations to take Taylor home. I was still
in the hospital with Taylor, while Roger was back home in Oakwood.
He had his daughter Danielle with him for the weekend, with plans to
come back up to Ann Arbor the following weekend.

We were busy over the next couple of days. A number of tests were
performed to make certain that Taylor was well enough to go home and
I completed the training required to get the apnea monitor. We were
really getting excited.

During our stay at Mott Children's Hospital, we'd made many
new friends from all over the United States, some of which we are still
in contact with. After spending weeks with the same people, who have
kids going through the same things, it's very easy to get to know each
other. After we parents left the hospital in the evening, we gathered at
Ronald McDonald House, talking and sharing with each other how the
day had gone. It was a great way of relaxing after a tense day spent with
our sick kids and the hospital hustle and bustle.

Finally, on July 6th, the day we had been praying for arrived! Roger
drove up to take us home. I already had the car there. Taylor and I
were going in the car and Roger was to follow us in the truck. We had
walkie-talkies so we could communicate easily while caravanning home.
I thought Taylor was acting odd and I kept telling the nurse about it,
asking if she was sure it was all right to take her home. She told me they

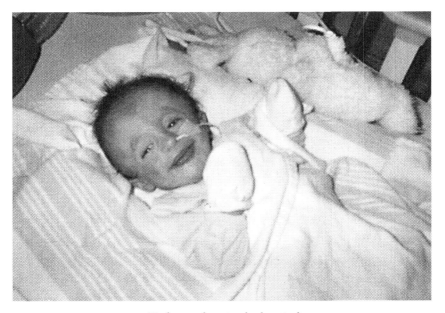

Taylor smiling in the hospital

wouldn't be letting Taylor go if she wasn't ready, so we said good-bye to the staff and our new friends. There was a lot of hugging each other and shared tears. Then we were on our way home.

We couldn't have been on the road for more than a half hour when Taylor started crying.

"Roger," I said over the walkie-talkie, "she won't stop crying and she feels hot."

He kept driving. "I'm sure she's okay," he said.

A little further on, I said, "Pull over. I'll try feeding her." But Taylor wouldn't eat; she just screamed. What a ride! It took forever. She cried all the way home and by the time we got there, my nerves were shot. I immediately checked her temp and sure enough, she had a fever of 102.7 degrees. I called back to the hospital. They told me to see how she did through the night and call back if the fever didn't break.

Michelle and Mitchell were waiting to greet us when we got home and Aunt Carolyn came to see us that evening. The night stretched out even longer than the trip home. We were up all night giving Taylor

Tylenol and sponge bathing her in an attempt to get her temperature to come down. I called the hospital back to let them know there had been no change. After that, I went ahead and took her to our local ER, where they called Life Flight to take her back to Michigan. Her fever had climbed to 105.5 and there was no doubt that something was seriously wrong.

Roger had plans to watch Danielle play softball that day. I told him to go ahead and go to the game and that I would go back to the hospital. I drove the car and while Taylor was transported in a squad. My foot pressed harder and harder on the accelerator until the car was practically flying, yet the Life Flight squad was going so much faster, they lost me in no time.

When I reached the hospital that we had just left the day before, Taylor was in the ER and the Life Flight team had just left, leaving Taylor a Life Flight bear to keep her company. She was admitted to a room and they started running tests.

She cried all night, and that just wasn't like Taylor. What could be wrong? I tried to calm her. She was given pain meds, but nothing helped. Then I noticed something unusual and in the early morning, I asked one of the nurses if she'd noticed how Taylor's heart rate monitor kept going up really high, out-of-this-world high. She watched and explained most likely there was a loose wire connection. She left the room and about five cardiologists came in on their regular rounds. The one we really liked, Dr. Ely, was there, and he voiced how surprised he was to see us back so soon. I explained to the doctors about how the heart rate numbers were shooting up high and then dropping back down. Right while I was telling them this, the monitor rocketed up to 269 beats per minute and Taylor's heart just stopped.

Once again it appeared that God had a part in our lives. Five cardiologists were already in the room the moment Taylor's heart stopped. They performed CPR, trying to get it going again. And once again, I was praying and crying. One of the physicians came over to me, put his arm around me, and told me it would be okay. It was the first time I was to see CPR being done on Taylor, and believe me, it was not something I ever wanted to see happen to my baby.

It took some time to get Taylor's heart beating again, but thank the good Lord, it did. Everything was up in the air again. They couldn't figure out why she had a fever and why her heart kept beating so erratically. As my brother Mike said, her heart was racing at Talladega speeds, and it didn't want to slow down to normal. When things finally began to settle down, I called Roger and asked him to please come up because I didn't want to be there by myself. I held it together and didn't tell him that Taylor's heart had stopped, because he had a long drive ahead and I didn't want him driving too fast and getting in an accident. When he arrived, I finally broke down.

I was worried it would happen again and that the next time they wouldn't be able to save her. I didn't want to stay in Michigan by myself, so Roger spent the night and the next day. Taylor's fever had resolved and her heart hadn't stopped again, so I told Roger we would be okay now and that he should go home and back to work.

Over the next couple of days, many tests were run and, luckily, Taylor slept through almost all of them. I was told it was residual from all fever reducers, plus the meds she'd been given for pain. All that stuff must have caught up with her because she slept for almost the entire two days. All the blood tests came back negative, and the results from the test for spinal meningitis came back negative, too. Her echocardiogram was also normal. What was to be done next?

We waited as Taylor recovered and hopefully got back to her regular self. I didn't want to take her home until I knew it was absolutely safe. Although I had questioned why she had been taken off digoxin after her surgery, I'd been told her heart was repaired, so she wouldn't need it anymore to control heart rate. It turned out she *did* need it and was put back on it. It seemed to keep her heart rate under control. I didn't know if it was the surgery, the digoxin, or both but it worked and that was what counted.

Eventually it was decided the fever might have been caused from bacteria on the pacer wires. Just to be sure, she was to stay for another

48 hours to see how she did. I was excited to think we just might get to go home again and soon.

Taylor was in a moderate care room, so I wasn't allowed to sleep in there with her. I didn't have a room at the Ronald McDonald House because we'd checked out when we went home. That left the waiting room. It was really dark in there and one of the other patient's dad was already sleeping in there. His little girl was on the general floor and his wife was in the room with her at night, while he stayed with their daughter during the day. Trying hard to be quiet and not disturb him, I made my bed on a foldout couch. He was on a little couch on the other wall. Since he didn't have a blanket, I very slowly and quietly took a blanket over to him and started to cover him up. He leaped up off that couch so fast!

I jumped back, saying, "I'm sorry! I thought you might want a blanket."

He smiled then, and said, "Thanks, I do."

After my heart stopped pounding in my chest, I tried to settle down and get some rest, but my mind just wouldn't shut down. Sleeping was a pretty hopeless endeavor because I couldn't stop thinking about Taylor.

Taylor spent two nights in moderate care before being moved to the general floor. And, as luck would have it, she was in the same room as that guy's daughter! I was so embarrassed, but he just laughed. They were really nice people. Their daughter was two years old and had just had heart surgery, too.

With Taylor back on digoxin, everything appeared to be proceeding smoothly. The results for her potassium check remained very high, but as it might have been from the way her blood had been drawn, it was retested. Her IV was placed in her head. I hated it because it looked awful. I was talking to the parents in the room with us while Taylor was lying in her bed. Her mobile was playing and she was watching it and jabbering. I happened to turn and look at her. The little mittens she wore on her hands to prevent her from pulling out her feeding tube were covered with blood. Blood was all over her pajamas and smeared on her face. I thought I was going to have a heart attack. I ran to her and she just looked up and smiled at me—definitely not in pain! She had pulled her IV out of her head. The staff decided not to put it back in because Taylor just messed with it and would not leave it alone. This was a good sign that she was getting back to her old self.

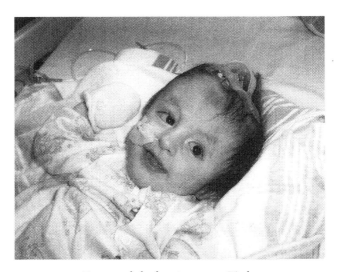

Even with little mittens on, Taylor
managed to pull out the IV on her head

CHAPTER 15

July 2006

I'd been with Taylor nonstop since she had been readmitted to Mott's. I fed her, bathed her, and administered her meds. Taylor couldn't speak for herself, so I had to be there for her. The staff knew I wanted to do those things for her, but one night, exhausted, I broke. A nurse came in at 3:00 a.m., woke me up, and handed me a bottle of formula for Taylor.

I said, "I don't mind doing what I can for her, but I can't stay awake for 24 hours every day."

She said, "I'll take her with me so you can sleep awhile."

After resting for a couple of hours, I went back to Taylor's room to find her crying.

The nurse said, "She wouldn't stop crying so I gave her an enema."

In addition to everything else since her heart surgery, Taylor had had severe diarrhea.

I said, "I hope you're kidding. She can't stop pooping and you gave her an enema?" When I told the doctor, he was very upset.

It was always difficult when it came time for Taylor's blood to be drawn for the various tests that were run. We learned early on that there were always the cowboy nurses who would say, *"I can get it. I'll bet you."* Those are the people that should have been prohibited from drawing blood. One time, after Taylor was poked seven times, not only had she been through enough, I'd had enough, too.

I said, "No more. Call the doctor."

They finally put in a central line and it was entered into her chart not to take blood from her veins. Sure enough, that same night, in came someone from lab saying he needed to draw blood. I told him it wasn't to be taken from her arms or legs. She was already black and blue all over her body from all the previous attempts. Her head, the tops of her hands, wrist, and even her ankles were bruised. The person from the lab told us the orders were from the doctor. I left the room and Roger stayed while they went ahead and poked her.

When the doctor came in I said, "I thought they weren't going to draw blood from her except from the line."

He said, "That's right."

We told him what happened.

He called the lab from Taylor's room and said, "I don't want anyone from the lab drawing Taylor's blood. You guys can't follow directions so the doctors will do it. Do not go back in her room. The poor baby looks like someone has beaten her."

That admission turned into another nine days in the hospital. When it was time to leave again, we repeated our good-byes. We hoped the second trip home would be a good one. And we wanted to be home for a longer span than 12 hours, like the last time.

On July 15th, I happily called Roger and announced we were coming home. What a sweetheart! He jumped in the truck and drove up to escort Taylor and I home. It made the trip a lot less scary knowing he was right behind us. That time Taylor slept all the way home. As I drove, I offered up a constant prayer of thanks: "Thank you, God, for letting us be in Michigan *when her heart stopped and for a team of five cardiologists to be in the room when it happened.*"

I knew it didn't have a thing to do with luck. It was God watching out for her.

Taylor came home on 13 different medications and I didn't want to get them mixed up. I asked Michelle again to provide me with some meds training. It was very confusing and I felt so much better when she was able to help. Since arriving home, Taylor continuously ran a low-grade fever. She didn't sleep much at night and sometimes she didn't sleep in the day either. I don't know how she was able to stay awake for such long periods of time. Although she'd racked up some record-breaking awake times, she also had some extremely long stretches of sleeping. Despite the fever, she was acting okay, but I knew something was up. I called the doctor and he said they would check her urine for the possibility of a urinary tract infection, but the results were clear. It just nagged at me—why did she have a fever?

Michelle came and stayed with Taylor while Layla and I went into town to get one of Taylor's prescriptions filled. Except for having a chance to spend some one-on-one time with my granddaughter, Layla, the trip was a waste of time. We had a good time together, but the pharmacist had to get in touch with the hospital in Michigan for instructions how to mix it.

Our first post-surgical appointment with Dr. Smith, Taylor's cardiologist, was scheduled for the end of July. I was excited to see his reaction to the sound of her repaired heart. She was not a happy girl that day and was fussy and whiny during the appointment. He said her chest might hurt and to give her some time to get over that. He suggested continuing the rotating doses of Tylenol and ibuprofen. He also decided to stop the thyroid med she'd been put on in Michigan, but it could take up to a week to get completely out of her system.

There's one less med for her to take. *Amen!* I thought. Taylor's weight remained at about 11 pounds. Results from the echo and blood work he'd ordered were fine, but her heart was still beating too fast. He sent us home and said he'd see us the next month.

My family reunion was coming up. It was to be held at our place. Some of my family came and helped us get ready by cleaning the barn and shop, mowing, and setting up a tent. My brother Mike, his wife Stacy, and their kids were driving up from Alabama. Since it turned out to be a very hot day, we kept Taylor in Roger's auto repair shop in her stroller. She was out of the blazing sun that way, and with the fans running, it was much cooler. Even with all the time required to give Taylor her treatments, feed and change her, it was a great day with the family all together.

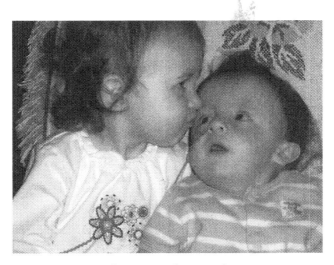

*Layla was very happy to have
her favorite playmate back home*

Taylor was sent home from the hospital in Ann Arbor with an apnea monitor. Up until then, I hadn't realized how scared I was to sleep. Since I didn't feel like I had to constantly watch her to see if she stopped breathing, I was finally able to relax and sleep a little, knowing if something was wrong, the alarm would go off. Little did I know that the times it did go off, it just about brought *my* heart to a standstill!

Taylor's low-grade fever ended up sending her back to the clinic for tests. Sure enough, she had a urinary tract infection (UTI) and had to go back on antibiotics for 10 days. Her regular pediatrician was moving to Germany to care for military children, so we began the search for a new doctor. It was not an easy task to find a physician willing to take on a complex case like Taylor. None of the other doctors Dr. Thread contacted had gotten back with him. I was talking to Kathy, the physician's assistant, and she said she would do some checking. She had success and called me at home to tell me we could meet with a Dr. Dawson and he would see what he could do.

He told us he could take her as a patient, but he had never had a Trisomy 18 case. He told us he would do his best and try everything he knew, but if he couldn't figure it out, Taylor would have to go on to Toledo. We agreed. I held Taylor the entire time during the first appointment with Dr. Dawson. He listened to her heart, checked her sinuses and blood oxygen level. He remarked on her small size and ran some tests. Over the years, Taylor had too many doctor appointments

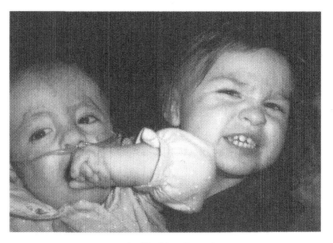

Layla "holding" Taylor

Taylor and Michelle enjoy some togetherness

to mention. Most of them were for typical kid ailments like runny noses and sinus infections, plus the many, many UTIs.

I will never forget the first time that I knew Dr. Dawson had really taken a liking to Taylor. I had her lying on the examining table waiting for him. When he came in, she followed with her eyes as he walked around the room. When he looked at her, making eye contact, she responded by smiling at him with the biggest, cutest smile ever. I believe this was the first time he really felt a connection to her and her to him.

† Chapter 16 †

August 2006

B y this time, I could tell right away if Taylor had a urinary tract infection. If her urine output decreased and it had a strong odor, I knew it was time for a urine culture. This happened so frequently, Dr. Dawson made what is called a "standing order" for the lab. If I thought something was up, I took a urine sample to the lab and they would call me with the results. That made it possible for us to start Taylor on antibiotics right away. It was a great help, because in addition to saving time, Dr. Dawson didn't want Taylor in the doctor's office if she didn't have to be. It was bad enough during our everyday lives, worrying about who around her might be sick or carrying a bug, and the worst place she could be was in a pediatrician's waiting room. Because he didn't want her picking up germs, he talked to me on the phone several times, as we decided if it was necessary to take her into the office or not. He ended up being one of our favorite doctors, and one who genuinely wanted to see her make progress.

Taylor had been battling diarrhea since her heart surgery—a complete turn around from the severe constipation she'd had since birth. One day I was alarmed to discover what I suspected was blood in her stool. I called Dr. Dawson's office and collected a sample to take in for testing.

He thought perhaps since we'd switched formulas several times in attempts to get her to gain weight, she might be having digestive problems. He said to give her nothing but Pedialyte—an electrolyte solution—for six hours, followed by a combination of half milk and half Pedialyte. By the time eight hours had passed, her stool appeared to be pure blood. I immediately took her to the local ER, where it was decided to send her on to Toledo. As arrangements were made for the squad to transport her, I made sure I had everything to go. With Taylor, we never traveled with just a bottle and diapers. We carried her meds, Pedialyte, formula, clothes, and a detailed list of what needed to be done at what time. I was taking inventory of what was in the bag, yet thinking about Taylor. *What could be wrong?*

I was completely lost in the depths of the diaper bag and my thoughts when I heard a voice say, "What is wrong with our baby Taylor?"

I looked up and there was Bonnie, a medic who runs for our town, along with my cousin Kirk. Bonnie was so sweet, I just started crying.

"I don't know what's wrong."

She assured me everything would be okay and said, "This kid's a fighter. This is just a setback."

She hugged me. I was glad and relieved Bonnie would be making the run with us. I rode in the front of the squad while Bonnie and another EMT were in the back with Taylor. Taylor just rode like she knew they would take good care of her. When we arrived at the hospital in Toledo, Bonnie stayed with us as long as she could. When it was time for the team to make their return trip, Bonnie gave me a hug and asked if there was anything she could do for us when she got back to town. I don't know if she knows how much it meant that she was with us that night and how appreciated her thoughtfulness was.

We were in the ER for hours before it was finally decided to admit her. When we went up to her room, we saw a lot of familiar faces, because we were getting very well acquainted with those people. When they saw her coming, everyone came to greet her. They made us feel so welcome.

"Here comes Baby Taylor," they all said.

It helped knowing people cared. As always, many tests were ordered, including a barium swallow. Barium was put into her feeding tube and observed under x-ray to see what happened. Once in, it takes two to three days to get it all out of her system. But, by the time it was out, we had a diagnosis. She had C-diff.

C-diff is short for clostridium difficile. A bacterial infection with C-diff causes severe diarrhea and can lead to a potentially fatal inflammation of the intestinal tract. It often occurs when people are on antibiotics for a long time and is extremely contagious, especially in healthcare facilities like hospitals and nursing homes. It's bad enough in a healthy adult, but in a tiny little girl like Taylor with all her other problems, it was a very serious situation.

Due to Taylor's ongoing need for antibiotics, it was only the first of nine times she would contract a C-diff infection. Already past the point of just diarrhea, we were told Taylor was in the last stages of the infection, that her colon was inflamed. Hearing this scared me so much, especially when we learned the treatment was another, stronger antibiotic! The cramping the new med caused made her cry a lot and she just felt bad in general. Every time after this, when that antibiotic was prescribed, I cringed, knowing her crying and inability to sleep meant we faced another challenging time. I felt so bad for her, but knew she needed the drug to get better.

While she was at the hospital in Toledo, she was evaluated to see if there was a reason behind all the urinary tract infections. A special colored liquid was put into her feeding tube. It was observed on a screen as it filled her bladder and as it emptied. It was very interesting to watch. The test revealed Taylor had an extra tube on her kidney that was non-functional. It was just there and didn't appear to cause any problems.

Three days later we went home.

The mystery of the unrelenting diarrhea Taylor had been experiencing since her heart surgery was solved with the C-diff diagnosis. Taylor was on the mend, but it was just our first experience with C-diff and the side effects from the powerful antibiotics needed to control it. Just as I learned the signs of a UTI, I quickly recognized when Taylor was starting with a C-diff infection. Taylor's C-diff bowel movements were extremely liquid and had a very distinct and unforgettable odor.

Dr. Dawson set up another standing order so we could also quickly test for the C-diff infection.

Taylor was sent to an endocrinologist to try and straighten out her abnormal magnesium and calcium levels.

The doctor we saw said, "Oh, sometimes this just happens. So we will just watch them."

At our next appointment with Dr. Smith, Taylor's cardiologist, I told him what the endocrinologist had said.

Dr. Smith said, "Absolutely not. You can go see Dr. Hotmire. He will figure it out. We're not just going to check it later. We need to know what's actually going on with kids that have the problems she has."

We went for our first appointment with Dr. Hotmire. We were waiting for him to come in the room when the door opened and a woman doctor came in.

"I knew it was you guys!" she said, as she hugged me and kissed Taylor.

"I've missed you so much."

It was the resident who had taken care of Taylor every time she had been in the hospital in Toledo. Whenever we were admitted there, even after a 24-hour shift, she'd come into Taylor's room and sit and talk with us. We only knew her as Dr. Jamie, but we felt like she was family. Dr. Jamie was doing her residency with Dr. Hotmire. She gave me her card so we could keep in touch. She moved on to her next hospital, and we didn't see her after that, but I sent her pictures of Taylor and kept her up to date on what was going on with her.

Taylor's C-diff seemed to be on hold for the moment, but she was often irritable. Since her heart surgery, she slept best during the day. I worked third shift when I was pregnant, so we figured she was definitely a third-shifter. She had the apnea monitor that allowed us to relax a little, but one night when Roger was working, that thing went off.

My heart dropped to my feet! I jumped out of bed and just stood there for a second, stunned. It was 3:00 a.m. There was no way to escape hearing that alarm. I wasn't fully awake or aware of what was going on. I discovered the alarm went off because the electrode stickers needed to be replaced. They wore off easily because she sweated so much. Talk about scaring me. . .that did it!

Taylor was scheduled to see Dr. Smith again. Her blood oxygen was 100 percent and her blood pressure was perfect. He was very happy about that and decided it was time to start spreading out our visits to every six months.

"Oh please, you can't do that to me! What if something happens?"

I begged and pleaded with him. He had seen Taylor every month since she was born.

"Kelly, I would never let her go every six months if I thought she wasn't ready." He tried to reassure me. "I'm going to have to wean you off these appointments," he added.

I was so afraid something would happen and we would lose her. I wasn't a cardiologist, but I did know he would never do anything to harm her. He was always one of our favorite doctors. So, instead of six months, her next appointment was scheduled for two months later. The next one was three months after that.

That was how Taylor's doctors were with their patients. They wanted to see them progress and it seemed especially true with Taylor and her Trisomy 18 diagnosis. It was a big thing for them to watch and be a part of her progress. Hers was a miracle story.

Around this time Taylor received a package from a woman we met while at the hospital in Ann Arbor. Through our stay there, we became very well-acquainted with her and she became as close as a family member. Her son, who was around 17 at the time, was a patient there, too. She made Taylor a gigantic afghan with Care Bears to match Taylor's Care Bears room at home. This woman's son wasn't expected to live more than five days and yet at the writing of this book, he's 21 years old. God does work in mysterious ways, I think.

† CHAPTER 17 †

September 2006

Taylor was beginning to recover from her long ordeal after surgery and I really wanted to take her outside. She was so cute and sweet; she was irresistible. And although just about everybody loved her, some people were intimidated by her differences. They were scared to hold her. And there were a few who pretended she didn't even exist. I was no different than anyone else with a baby, and those kinds of attitudes didn't stop me from wanting people to see her. She existed and I wasn't trying to hide her. Plus, most people *wanted* to see her. When we did go out, friends and acquaintances came right over to us, wanting to know all about Taylor's latest developments. Seeing her, I believe, gave people hope. They knew we'd been told she wouldn't be here one day, yet more than a year later, there she was. Hearing what a little fighter she was and how well she did was very important to them. They believed, just as we did, that our Taylor was a living miracle. God really did have a hand in Taylor's creation.

It was our second Labor Day since Taylor arrived. We took her uptown for the homecoming festivities. I even entered the baking contest with my zucchini bread and won first place! I was so excited because I had not won before. That month, we decided to head to a neighboring county for their annual fair, but that trip didn't turn out as I had hoped. As Roger, Danielle and I pushed Taylor around in her stroller, she cried most of the time. I felt so bad for her. We just needed to get her back home—where she was most comfortable and spent practically all her time.

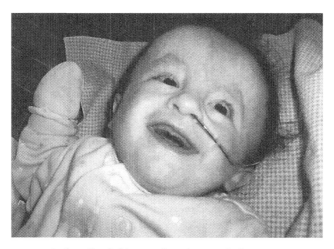

God really did have a hand in Taylor's creation

We went back to Toledo to see Dr. Hotmire, the endocrinologist. Taylor's blood test results indicated her blood calcium level was still too high. We were to give her as little vitamin D as possible, but this was a very difficult order to follow. Most people's bodies require a lot of vitamin D. We read every label and found that it's added to just about everything. It was a big challenge to find food products without it. Even cereal, a food we were just starting her on, had vitamin D added. She didn't really like the cereal, but she needed the added calories and the doctor hoped it would help her gain weight. He also told me that although her calcium was at a high level, it wasn't settling in her joints, which was good. He said he had talked to Dr. Dawson and they both agreed that she should see an infectious disease specialist, so she was sent to Dr. Bradshaw.

Taylor was now one year, four months old, and weighed 10 pounds, eight ounces. I raised her formula intake to 30 calories an ounce. While she was in the hospital in Michigan, she had been given an additive called Polycose in her milk to add calories, but it was so rich, she couldn't tolerate it for long. After a few weeks of it added to her formula, she cried and cried. Once, when I gave it to her for three days in a row, she cried for 17 hours! I took her to the doctor and he said it was probably too rich for her stomach. Although we wanted so badly for Taylor to gain weight, we learned we just couldn't push her little body. It was going to take time.

She finally began gaining weight at a good rate, but we really didn't know why. I didn't know and the doctors didn't know. I was happy, at least until I called to tell Taylor's cardiologist's nurse so she could tell Dr. Smith the good news. She didn't celebrate along with me.

She said, "Kelly, she can't gain more than one ounce a day."

"What!" I was shocked at this.

"This gain could mean bad weight," she continued. "Have her pediatrician check her out. After heart surgery, that weight could be water around her heart. You have to watch it very closely."

Taylor's weight had climbed to 11 pounds, four ounces, which sounded great to me, but perhaps it wasn't such good news after all.

When I called Dr. Dawson's office, he said, "What I want you to do is weigh her Saturday, Sunday, and Monday and then call with the weights."

She continued to gain over the weekend. Dr. Dawson told me to bring her in so they could check her out.

At the appointment, he looked at her and said, "She looks great. She sounds great after listening to her heart and chest. If this were bad weight, she would look very puffy and she doesn't." He continued, "She actually looks like she's getting a double chin and her legs are finally looking like chicken legs. That is wonderful. You do such a great job with her, Kelly."

"I try," I said, "but I worry a lot."

He said, "I would be worried about you if you didn't."

It made me feel so good to know that her doctor noticed my efforts. It meant so much.

I asked him, "Do I drive you crazy?"

He replied, "I wish all my parents were like you."

Taylor was scheduled for a sedated MRI (magnetic resonance imaging) to check the bend in her back. She slept in the car all the way to Toledo. She should have—she'd been up all night! We asked the tech if they could try it with her just sleeping, because when Taylor was out, she was out. After being up all night, we couldn't wake her and if we didn't have to have her anesthetized, it would be wonderful. The tech said we could try it and, just like an angel, Taylor didn't budge throughout the entire test. They directed me to stand by her and hold her arms straight up and she didn't move a muscle. Once the MRI results were read, an appointment would be scheduled to discuss the results with Dr. Brown. So, three days later, we were back to Toledo. Dr. Brown said the bend had actually improved. Before it was 58 degrees and now it was 55 degrees, but we still needed to get her back into the brace.

Fortunately we had the brace with us. Because of Taylor's weight increase, it would no longer close. We needed to go to Don's office so he could lengthen the Velcro strips that held it closed. Taylor hated the restriction of that brace. As soon as we put it on her, she started to fuss. I know it was tight and hot. But the doctor said it had been long enough after her surgery and she needed it to help prevent the bend in her spine from worsening. She was supposed to wear it 23 hours a day, but that didn't happen. It was too painful for both of us, but I tried to have it on her as much as I could.

It was Christmas time! Dr. Smith and the other pediatric cardiologists throw a big Christmas party every year for their patients. It was held in Toledo at the Imagination Station, a science museum for kids. It is really neat they do this for their patients and their families. We really wanted to take Taylor, so Roger, Danielle, Hailey, my cousin Cheryl's daughter, and I went. Hailey also sees Dr. Smith for a heart condition.

We had a great time! Around 4,000 kids were invited. That's a lot of kids, parents, and siblings gathered in one building. Dr. Smith was surprised and glad to see Taylor there.

As it was cold and flu season, it was time for Taylor's first RSV (respiratory syncytial virus) immunization. It is given to small babies to help prevent a certain type of severe respiratory infection that can be fatal.

The nurse came in and said, "I don't want to give this to her, but the doctor ordered it." She just kept looking at Taylor and then she stuck it in her leg. Taylor had dealt with so much pain and had so many pokes that she never made a sound, not one. She was a real trooper. She ran a low-grade fever that night, I believe, from the shot.

We went to the appointment that had been made with Dr. Bradshaw, the infectious disease doctor. Her office was in Toledo, right across the hall from Taylor's doctors, Smith and Hotmire. How convenient for us!

Dr. Bradshaw said in her 26 years of practice she had never seen anyone have C-diff continuously for six months. The Flagyl, the medicine that made her very irritable, should have kicked it the first time. Taylor had also been on Vancomycin, and that should have taken care of anything the Flagyl didn't. So, once again, the tests began. Dr. Roberts, the one who had first diagnosed Taylor with C-diff, was helping Dr. Bradshaw try to solve the mystery.

When he walked in, he looked at Taylor and said, "Don't tell me she still has C-diff?"

They ran all kinds of tests and he asked us to make an appointment at his Lima office, a lot closer for us, so we could discuss it and get to the bottom of it.

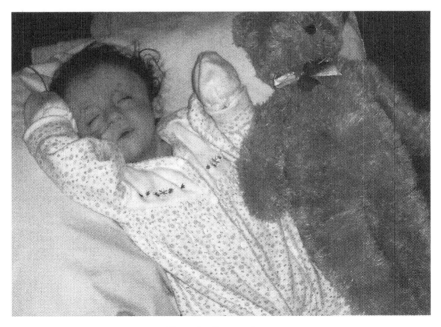

Sound asleep at home

CHAPTER 18

December 2006 through July 2007

A couple weeks later, we went to Lima for the appointment. Because we had a hard time finding his office and I thought we were going to be late, I was quite upset by the time we got there. Michelle called my cell phone and when I answered, it was obvious I was frustrated. Fortunately, she had done some of her nursing nearby so she was able to direct us over the phone. Roger called the office and told them we were going to be late.

Life with Taylor was very complicated and stressful. When I became frustrated by it all, it was even worse. Little things like being late easily aggravated me. We finally found the place and they were so nice.

When Taylor was in the hospital in Ann Arbor, she had been prescribed magnesium. While there, she took 8 ml of it, four times a day. By the time we left for home after her surgery, the dose was down to 4 ml, four times a day. Dr. Roberts said this dose was too high and way too much for her tiny body to handle. He also told us the magnesium and acidophilus, a helpful digestive bacteria, could both cause diarrhea. As a result, she needed to be taken off the magnesium. Her dose was gradually lowered, first down to 3.5 ml, four times a day, for ten days. Then her blood was checked to make sure it was staying in the normal range. After that, she took 3 ml, four times a day. Her blood was checked in ten days and so on. It took along time, but he got her down to 2 ml, four times a day. She would remain on the acidophilus. Dr. Roberts also took her off Reglan. She continued to have diarrhea, but not as bad. We hoped the changes in her meds would help the C-diff clear up. However, since it lay dormant in her system until something triggered it to grow again—like the antibiotics—it continued to be a problem for Taylor.

My son Mitchell's girlfriend and I started researching magnesium on the Internet and found that magnesium supplements work best when taken with food. We thought perhaps it could be given with Taylor's cereal, but she needed four doses a day. We tried it, but there was no way she could consume that much cereal four times a day. So that test failed.

We went to my Aunt Carolyn's for Christmas and also to Roger's sister's house. Taylor cried a lot at Roger's sister's house, as if she didn't feel well. Because of that, we thought we'd make it a quick stop at Aunt Carolyn's house, but ended up staying longer. Two of Taylor's favorite people were at Aunt Carolyn's—Rhonda and my cousin Diana's husband, Ron. Ron always loved kids and was never intimidated by Taylor. As soon as we walked into a dinner or gathering with Taylor, he offered to hold her so I could have a chance to get something to eat.

That day, I don't think I held her but once. She laughed out loud, which caused everyone to laugh.

It was the cutest thing to hear her laugh. Michelle could make her laugh all the time because she interacted with her all the time. Taylor loved her big sister, Michelle. Gary could get a smile out of Taylor, any time, day or night. She really responded well to him. With her big brother Mitchell, it was different. He was a guy and he liked kids, but he liked them to be able to walk, and talk, and play. I think Taylor overwhelmed him a little. But still, if he came in and she was just yelling, he would say, "What are you yelling about? Won't Mom help you? Sometimes you have to throw a fit then she'll do it. You're going to have to be madder than that." I think she was just too small for Danielle and with so much going on with her, she kind of intimidated her too.

One day, Mitchell and my nephew, Cody, were sitting with Taylor and me in the living room. She was in her chair in front of the TV and

Taylor at Christmas 2006

suddenly she just started cracking up laughing. They thought it was so funny, they burst out laughing, too.

They asked her, "What's so funny, Taylor?"

They had never heard her laugh out loud for that long. It was adorable. Cody had held Taylor a couple times, but only for pictures. Since Cody had a baby of his own, it was a little different for him. He was separated from his girlfriend and stayed with Roger, Taylor, and I for about a year. It was nice because someone was there with me at night in case of an emergency. Mitchell had an apartment located in another small town, just two miles away, and Michelle lived in the same town. If I needed them, they could get here within a couple minutes.

At Christmas, Taylor weighed 12 pounds, one ounce, which was the most she ever weighed. She made the move up to six-to-nine-months sized clothes at one year and six months old. Amazing.

Dr. Hotmire's office called. Taylor's calcium was at 10.6 mg/dL. They considered 13 dangerous for her. When she went to Michigan for heart surgery, it was 17.6. He found that the calcium levels could be kept at a normal level if she was well hydrated. He suggested we give her 50 cc of water and 50 cc of the electrolyte solution, Pedialyte, every day. He wanted her levels checked every three months. This did the trick to keep her calcium at normal levels. As a result of that extra 100 cc of fluid, however, we couldn't continue to increase her milk intake. It seemed she just couldn't get a break, but high levels of calcium were too dangerous, so we simply had to hope for the best.

Dr. Hotmire suggested we start trying her on foods in addition to cereal. So we ventured into the wonderful world of vegetables. She liked squash, sweet potatoes, and carrots, but absolutely hated the green stuff like green beans and peas. When I did feed her the green beans or peas, she spit them back at me. Sometimes I ended up wearing more than what she had eaten.

I was feeding her one day while Mitchell was there. Each time I gave her a bite, she shook her head again and again: no!

Mitchell finally said to me, "She doesn't want them. Can't you understand no?"

I laughed as she just looked at me as if to say, "Yes, listen to him. I don't want them."

Taylor didn't talk but she got her message across!

It was time for another appointment with Dr. Smith, her cardiologist. She hadn't seen him at the office for three months and I couldn't wait to see if it was good news or bad news. He told us that Taylor still had mild pulmonary stenosis, meaning the pulmonary valve in her heart was still not completely normal, but other than that, her blood pressure was perfect, her blood oxygen level was 99 percent, and her weight had increased. He had changed her heart medicine to Atenolol and she had handled that very well. That was good news. He was very happy about the progress.

He said, "Okay, this is it. Bring her back in six months."

I said, "Great! We'll see you then."

I'm sure he was surprised I didn't fight it or whine, because it would be so long between visits and it made me nervous. I knew he wouldn't have done it if he thought she wasn't ready.

Next we needed to contact the dentist to ask about Taylor. She was one year and eight months old, but had not gotten any teeth. There was absolutely no sign of them either and I was beginning to worry. He said to bring her in and he would see if she was going to get teeth or not. I had no idea.

Of course, when we went for her appointment, she had been up all night and was sound asleep. She slept through the entire visit and didn't move or make a noise while he took x-rays.

He said, "That's the best patient I ever had."

He looked at the x-rays and said, "Kelly, guess what? She has a whole mouth full of teeth just waiting to break through."

I was so excited. Now at least we knew.

He said, "The reason her teeth haven't broken through is because she doesn't chew on toys and bite on the spoon when she eats."

Everything with Taylor was just waiting and seeing what happened. I put her on a website for Trisomy 18 and talked with other parents. They really helped a lot and I met such nice people who were willing to share their stories with me. I got so much information from them that I hadn't read about before. I'm so glad I put her on that site.

She was about 23 months old when I found that her first tooth had finally come in. They seemed to pop in after that and within about seven months, she had all the teeth she was going to get. It was amazing! I've never seen anything like it.

She was a miracle, all right. God helped her get that far. She was now yelling at the top of her lungs all the time. I think she just liked to hear herself. I could only laugh. The child they said would never smile, coo, or track things, had a big attitude and an even bigger personality. What a kid!

*Taylor in her Ohio State outfit, sent to Dr. Smith and Taylor
in her specially made outfit sent to Dr. O'Malley*

CHAPTER 19

August 2007 through April 2008

Taylor developed a cough that never seemed to go away. At times it seemed to calm down, then it would sneak back up on us. She was taking medicine for the cough, but it just wouldn't go away. I finally got tired of all the medicines and called Dr. Dawson. He said to bring her in because that cough should've been gone. He decided to put her on breathing treatments, saying she had gunk that she just couldn't cough up, maybe due to allergies. He thought the treatments might help clear it out. When Taylor coughed, it wasn't like other kids. She could never bring the phlegm all the way up. It would be right there and then it would go back down. Dr. Dawson thought the treatments might loosen it better and help her to cough it up.

When it was time for a treatment, she just threw a fit.

I had Roger give them to her when he had time because she seemed better for him than for me. She would squirm all over and yell at me, but for Roger, she was almost always an angel. Go figure!

I will be the first to admit, I do just what I have to around the house. Instead of dusting and scrubbing and sweeping, I spent my time holding Taylor, or simply sitting and watching her. When I talked to her, she engaged with me, watched me, and sometimes laughed. To me, these were amazing things. We had always been told she may not recognize our faces or voices. We discovered very

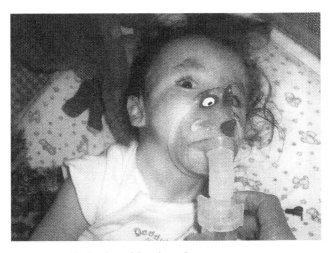

Taylor hated her breathing treatments!

early on that she was very well aware of who we were. She was an amazing kid.

One day when I was watching her sleep, I noticed her lips kept turning a bluish-purple color. After that, I couldn't stop watching her. After her lips turned dusky, they always went back to their normal pink, but I wondered why it was happening. At first I thought it might be my imagination. But we couldn't ignore it, so I made an appointment with Dr. Smith. I reported to him what I had observed. He hooked her up to a machine to check her blood oxygen level. It dropped very low, around 65 percent. A normal level is 97 to 100 percent.

He said, "Something isn't right. She doesn't seem to be getting enough oxygen, yet she looks completely normal, like nothing's going on. She's not gasping for air or waking up. We need to talk to a pulmonologist."

He continued, "She has a valve that wasn't working right, and her pulmonary stenosis has worsened. We can't let this go; she already has so much going on."

As a result, Dr. Smith called Dr. Dawson. Dr. Dawson said his office would schedule an appointment with Dr. Veer. Apparently getting in to see him required magical powers, because we couldn't get an appointment until two months later! Dr. Dawson's response was to get Dr. Veer on the phone. (He had trained with him.) Dr. Dawson got on the phone with him and, boom, she had an appointment in a week.

My cousin Rhonda and I took Taylor and headed for Toledo to see Dr. Veer. He said Taylor needed a test that would record her oxygen levels and breathing patterns. It was to be done in our home because it took at least 12 hours to complete. The equipment arrived the next day. The technicians came in, showed me how to run the machine and how to read it. A thin piece of plastic taped under Taylor's nose would monitor her oxygen levels and her breathing patterns. After the readings began, I couldn't believe my eyes. Her oxygen dropped down to around 60 percent, which is very low. No wonder her lips were turning blue!

After reviewing the results of the monitoring, Dr. Veer decided to try supplemental oxygen on Taylor while she slept. With the delivery of the tanks the next day, I had more machines to learn how to run and I had to get accustomed to an entirely new set of alarm beeps and buzzes. In addition to that, we were told to always keep her on the apnea monitor, because oxygen deprivation could cause her heart rate to drop or stop. Each time her oxygen level did drop, the episode always lasted for at least 128 seconds.

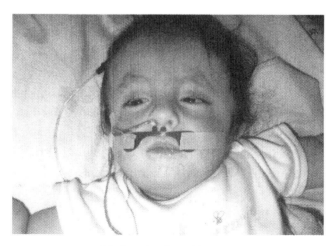

Undergoing breathing tests

Just as Taylor's machines were her constant companions, once again worry became mine. I said a lot of prayers to keep me going. I asked God to help me understand and to know what to do if something happened.

The day after, we had to take Taylor back to Toledo Hospital for more tests. Dr. Veer was worried Taylor might be having seizures because her oxygen was now dropping as low as 33 percent. She was to undergo a bronchoscopy. It was performed by inserting a tiny camera at the end of a long, thin, lighted tube to see what was causing her breathing problems.

Dr. Veer said Taylor truly was a miracle and that they would work as quickly as possible to discover what the problem was so they could help her continue to progress. Sleep apnea was ruled out, but her oxygen levels were at such dangerously low levels at times, he feared she was having seizures.

When I told Dr. Dawson of the findings, he asked, "Are you sure? Thirty-three percent is very, very low." When he got the report he was floored about the low numbers.

During the bronchoscopy, Dr. Veer found that Taylor had severe acid reflux, saying her esophagus was really torn up. He also found bacteria in her lungs, which was not uncommon with acid reflux. As a result of those findings, Dr. Dawson was called and asked if Taylor could be switched from the antibiotic she was currently taking for her chronic UTIs to another that would be more effective on the lung infection. We found out the new medicine could successfully treat both infections. The next step was to get Taylor into see a neurologist. I told him I refused to take her to the one that we found to be so negative. He asked who it was and then said, "No, no, I am sending her to Dr. Coty. He's very nice. You'll like him."

As a precaution, Dr. Coty, the neurologist immediately started Taylor on an antiseizure medicine. He also scheduled her to have a video electroencephalogram (EEG) that would require a three-day hospital stay and someone to be awake with her for the entire 72 hours. I told him I'd give it my best shot, but that I wasn't sure I'd be able to stay awake that long.

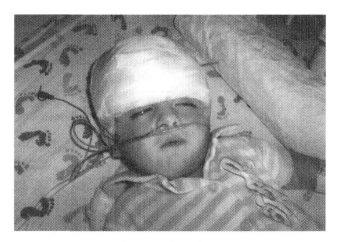

Undergoing the video EEG

It was our decision if the test was run, but I knew Roger felt the same way I did—we hadn't come that far just to give up.

While she was hooked up to the monitor it was discovered that she was starting to get a sinus infection so she was prescribed Zithromax, another antibiotic, for five days. The test came back negative for seizures. Through all of this Taylor had continued to gain and her weight was well over 13 pounds. Praise the Lord!

While we were at the hospital for the EEG, Michelle called me.

"I'm not supposed to tell you, but I knew you would want to know that they just took Tim [my brother] by Life Flight to a Seattle hospital because he has a crushed vertebra and is in surgery."

He had been in an accident and when my sister-in-law called and told Michelle, she said she thought I'd enough to deal with and to wait until we got home. But my older daughter knew me very well and knew I would want to know. Within a few days of all this, the pastor of my church died unexpectedly at the age of 51. He had done a lot of praying for Taylor. He was missed.

We continued to see Dr. Coty because Taylor needed to be weaned off the seizure meds. In Dr. Coty's office for an office visit, I realized you meet all kinds of people. Kids are the best. I was sitting in the office and a little boy about four or five was just down from us. Taylor was in her stroller, and the boy came down and sat by me, saying, "What are you doing lady?" His grandma asked, "Is he bothering you?" and I said, "Absolutely not. He's fine." We talked and soon he got up and looked in the stroller, asking, "Hey lady, why does your baby have a hose in her nose?" I started laughing, and his grandma came running, saying, "I'm so sorry." I said I would rather him ask than wonder what's wrong with her. Kids are the most honest people you will ever talk to. After about a year she was cleared from Dr. Coty's care.

It was the end of September and we hadn't been home long before I had to call Dr. Dawson to see her. She was coughing and I feared it was the beginning of pneumonia. I was right. Her chest x-rays revealed she had a very cloudy lung which was the start of pneumonia. She was still on an antibiotic for C-diff and now this. She truly had to be one of the toughest kids I've ever seen. Once again her meds were changed around

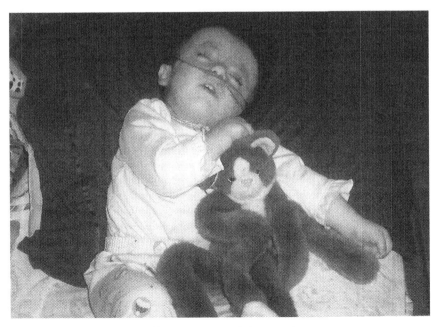

Taylor snoozing with her monkey

and she was put on new ones for a longer period of time. Follow-up x-rays would be taken the following week.

Then we were off to see Dr. Brown, the orthopedist. Her back was x-rayed and the news couldn't have been much worse. She had a severe case of scoliosis. Taylor's bend in her spine had increased from 53 to 75 degrees, indicating it was time for surgery. Dr. Brown wanted to put an extendable rod in her back. Normally this meant that every six months additional surgery would be required to lengthen the rod so it would "grow" with her. He told us since her growth rate was so slow she may not need it lengthened that often. He was to consult with her pulmonologist and cardiologist because they would all have to be in agreement that she was strong enough to survive another surgery. They would also have to decide where the surgery should take place. It was possible that we'd have to go back to Michigan where she had her heart surgery. Dr. Brown was almost certain her oxygen problem was caused by her spine crushing her lungs and that it would soon begin crushing her heart, so we had to move fast.

So many details had to be attended to before Taylor could have the spinal surgery. It was going to take time. Because she was so small, Dr. Brown had to have a steel rod made especially for Taylor. He told us he had hoped she could wait for surgery until she was ten or eleven years old. But, obviously, that was not going to be an option.

I thought, *What more could she possibly have to go through?* Then I remembered what my mom always told me: *"Never ask what can happen next."* My mother was a smart woman.

† CHAPTER 20 †

May 2008 through October 2008

Roger and I own a 24-hour auto wrecker service and that required someone to run it while we were at the hospital with Taylor. Our friends Dean and Cheryl ran it for us whenever we had to be away. It would have been very difficult if I'd had to stay at the hospital without Roger because he had to stay home for the business. He would have had to constantly run back and forth, and I didn't want to be there alone with Taylor and be solely responsible for all the decisions that arose during her stay.

Cheryl also made it possible for Roger and me to frequently attend church services on Sundays because she came and stayed with Taylor. When the weather was bad or it was flu season, it was impossible for us to take Taylor out. She just couldn't be exposed to people who might be ill.

One of my daughter Michelle's friends, Verda, asked about having a benefit for Taylor through a nationally known nonprofit organization begun by noted artist P. Buckley Moss. The group from northwestern Ohio is named Trees of Life. Each year they hold a benefit for someone who has special needs because of disabilities or other medical conditions. Funds were raised through the sale of raffle tickets. When Taylor got a little bigger, she was going to need a special bed, chair, and wheelchair and they would come with big price tags. After the ticket sales were tallied up, it ended up being the biggest the group had ever had. It showed us that people just wanted to help.

Bonnie, our friend who was a member of the Oakwood EMS and had been so helpful and supportive, was at a local festival with her son. He spotted a poster with Taylor on it advertising the Trees of Life benefit raffle tickets. He wanted to buy some tickets. He knew Taylor and thought she was cute. He had helped Bonnie babysit for her before and he had Taylor smiling all that night.

In the meantime, Dr. Veer gave his okay for Taylor to undergo a sedated CAT scan. When she saw Dr. Smith for her six-month cardiology checkup, he had no idea we were going to approach him about his giving her permission for the spinal surgery. We went in with a tray of his favorite treats that I had baked. I told him of the orthopedist's findings and said we needed to know if he, too, would give his consent.

He said, "Yes, she'll do fine. I don't see why not. Do I still get the goodies?"

We laughed so hard. I couldn't believe it had been that easy. Dr. Smith also believed that we really didn't have any other option. If her spine began to put pressure on her heart, that would be the end. She'd gone through too much to allow that to happen. His only concern was getting her off the ventilator after surgery.

"She's a tough kid," he said. "But they are going to have to be hard on her. If she's taken off the ventilator and they put her back on because they think she can't do it, she will never come off it."

He continued, "She can do it, but she is so small and some people just don't understand what a fighter she is. They may feel sorry for her, but Taylor doesn't want sympathy, nor will she take it."

Some of Taylor's doctors thought we were crazy when we consulted an herbalist. Under his direction, we had been applying a mixture of herbal oils to her back for about eight months. Did it help? All we knew was that the bend in her spine had not increased in that time period. We didn't care what anyone thought. Roger and I had to know we had done everything we possibly could to prevent the necessity for surgery.

But, once again, the curvature began to get worse. When I called the herbalist, he told me she must have gotten a virus, but at least it had prolonged the inevitable. In the end, we were glad we did it.

Dr. Brown wanted Taylor to gain more weight before the surgery. Michelle suggested we put her back on night feeds through the nasalgastric tube. Dr. Brown agreed to this and a pump was ordered and delivered to the house.

It was at this time that the worst of my worries became reality. Early one morning, around 4:00 a.m., Taylor's apnea monitor alarm sounded. I jumped up and rushed to her. I could see by the small light I always kept on at her bedside that her lips were purple. I turned on a brighter light and she didn't respond. She was motionless. A prayer automatically generated itself. *God, please let me know what to do. Please let me know what to do.* Even with the completion of CPR classes, I was scared. I picked up her limp body and shook her. Not hard, but it was enough. She gasped for air and began crying. Then I began crying.

There was no sleep for me the rest of that night as I fretfully waited for Roger to get home from his night shift.

This was about the same time Mitchell's girlfriend moved in with us. I was so happy and relieved that I would have someone with me in case of an emergency. It really lessened some of the incredible stress I'd been living under. I had always made sure I had a phone with a speaker in case I had to talk and give CPR at the same time. But now there were two of us: one to communicate and one to tend to Taylor.

Taylor was at her highest weight ever. Drum roll. . .15 pounds, 12 ounces! Even while still battling the C-diff, she had somehow managed to gain weight. That had never happened before.

We needed to take Taylor to Toledo to see her orthopedist, Dr. Brown. He was going to begin putting a series of casts on her feet. Because she never stood on her feet, she developed a condition called drop foot—her feet were turned down and out. The plan included having five sets of casts on her feet that would gradually turn them back to a normal position. After the cast treatment was completed, she would wear braces that went from her knees to her toes.

Taylor had a bad UTI the day she was to receive her first set of casts. She was on some strong meds and didn't want to be held or even looked at. Needless to say she wasn't happy about the long ride, either. But we made it. The casts were applied without incident. When we got home, however, I thought one cast looked like it was lower on her leg than it had been when it was applied. Sure enough, the next morning when I woke up and checked on Taylor, there laid the cast in her bed. She had somehow managed to wiggle it off. She lay there kicking that leg up and down and had the biggest smile on her face.

When I called Dr. Brown, he laughed and said some kids can manage to get them off, and although he hadn't expected Taylor to, good for her.

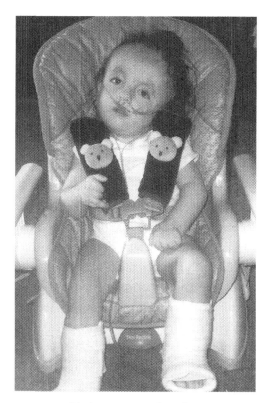

Taylor sitting in her chair
wearing her foot casts

"She's got a lot of spunk," he said. "We will just put another one on next week."

After five sets of casts it was time for braces. They are called AFOs. There were all sorts of designs to choose from, so we picked pink toys with purple Velcro straps. They were so cute, but she hated them. It didn't take her long to figure out how to slide them off her legs. Sometimes at night she worked so hard at getting them off, I took them off so we could both get some sleep. I finally found that putting two pairs of socks on her feet slowed her down.

I don't know why we thought she would keep the AFOs on. The first day she wore them, she took one off three times. At her next appointment with Dr. Brown he called her a "little Houdini."

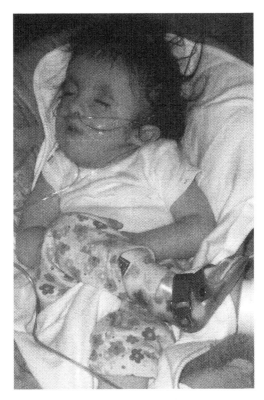

Taylor's pink and purple AFOs

In addition to the leg braces, we had other issues to attend to. Taylor's physical therapist and I had been searching for a stroller and a chair for her. Even though she couldn't hold her head up, sit up, stand, or crawl, we thought if she was placed into a sitting position, it might help to strengthen her neck muscles. I found a chair in Toledo that had a five-point harness. Taylor loved that chair because she could recline or sit up and see everything. Plus, I could move her from room to room easily. We couldn't leave her there for long periods of time, however. She couldn't move herself around very well, so we needed to reposition her about every hour to prevent pressure sores.

Taylor was always a very determined little girl. Her yelling had to be about the funniest. I think she just talked because she liked to hear herself. Sometimes when she got wound up, she would get really loud, especially in church. As soon as the preacher started talking, so did Taylor.

One Sunday, he said to the congregation, "I love the competition, Taylor."

Taylor made me laugh every day—and it was what I needed. She just made my day.

CHAPTER 21

November 2008 through January 2009

At the very end of January we had an appointment with Taylor's orthopedist. The x-rays showed the curve in her back had changed very little since October. What great news! Dr. Brown said he wanted to see her weekly. He warned us that she had a very big curve and he might have to schedule surgery soon.

When we went to the next appointment he was happy again to report very little change. We were to return for another visit in a week.

In the meantime, Taylor got her new chair so she could sit up. She had been getting physical and occupational therapy from Angie since she was one year old. She began preschool with Deedi and speech therapy with Beth when she was three. Her head control appeared to be better and she began to participate more. We were to see Dr. Brown in mid-November and her cardiologist on November 25th. The hope was that he would be able to discontinue her heart medication.

The news wasn't good. After months where there had been very little change in the degree of bend in her back, it jumped from 71 to 92 degrees. Originally the plan had been that we would start planning for surgery when it reached 80. But in a very short four-month period it had leaped right past that mark. Everything changed. There were so many concerns when it came to Taylor. We had to consult Dr. Smith, her cardiologist, about her heart condition, and her pulmonologist to get his okay. Her weight, or lack of it, was a major concern. Because she was so little and thin, the steel bars implanted during the back surgery could rub through her skin and trigger infection. And, not only had the curvature of her spine increased, her backbone was beginning to twist. If it continued to do so, it could have pinched off her spinal cord and she wouldn't be able to move her legs again.

Dr. Brown suggested we plan for the surgery to take place in a month, giving us time to get a little more weight on Taylor and work out insurance issues. He also explained to us that the curve of her spine might be the cause of her inability to get over sinus infections. Her lungs had become so compressed she couldn't cough up secretions properly. We already knew if it began to press on her heart, we were looking at big trouble. The one bright spot in all of this was that the braces were doing a great job straightening Taylor's feet.

When we went to Dr. Smith, the cardiologist, it was a good news-bad news scenario. The echogram showed that her heart looked better than the last time, six months earlier. Blood pressure, blood oxygen level, heart rate—all perfect. He said she looked good and her color was good. At Michelle's suggestion, due to Taylor's continuous coughing, he listened to her lungs and said let's do x-rays just to see what's going on. An x-ray was done just to make sure and sure enough, she had the start of pneumonia and was started on antibiotics, again. We didn't need another set of x-rays to tell us she was getting better, because she was finally happy again, smiling ear to ear and back to her exuberant yelling and noise-making self. The x-rays showed significant improvement.

As we continued on our journey toward surgery, Taylor had an appointment with a pulmonologist. He told us Taylor looked good on the outside, not so much on the inside. He wanted to move up the date of the surgery, fearing that her spine, because it was so close to the lung at this point, might puncture it.

It was a very dangerous situation and we were out of choices. If she didn't have the surgery, she didn't have a chance. She was a tough little girl, but there was a real chance she might never get off the ventilator. We had been told that about her heart surgery, too. The doctor told us we might be faced with the decision of turning off the machine. I told him I knew that. I said I didn't want Taylor to live life in constant pain. The doctor told me she was already in a lot of pain, but it was just another day for her. But even with all she had going on, he thought she was the happiest little girl he'd ever seen. And Taylor just smiled at him.

We prayed that God would get us through yet another trial. I wasn't about to give up, because Taylor never had. We were so thankful for everyone who had been with us through it all and who continued to hold us up in their prayers and to be there for us.

My cousin Rhonda went with Taylor and me for Taylor's bronchoscopy. The doctor wasn't happy with the results and changed his mind about going forward with the surgery. He was worried that the flap that closed off her airway, called the epiglottis, wouldn't work after she was taken off the ventilator because she would be so heavily sedated. It meant she could end up needing a tracheotomy. The flap not working right was not a new thing for Taylor. It could cause problems without the surgery and I would have much rather it happen when she was in the hospital.

"This is not a good way of life," he said. "And it means 20 times more work for you."

I just couldn't give up. I said, "I'll do whatever I have to do to take care of her."

Of course, he wasn't familiar with Taylor—how far she'd come. If we had listened to everything we'd been told to do or not do about Taylor, she would have been gone a long time before that. I didn't want her to have a poor quality of life, but we needed to offer her a chance. I couldn't live with myself if we didn't at least give her a chance. I couldn't say no to her only option of survival based on "what ifs." We knew all the risks from when she had her heart surgery. My gut feeling was to go ahead with it.

It was the end of January and we were still working out a lot of details such as a sedated MRI, blood work, meetings with the physicians, and paperwork. Taylor's spinal surgery was finally scheduled for March 9, 2009. She had been well and her weight was stable at

16 pounds, six ounces. And once again, Taylor achieved a milestone all the experts said she would never reach: she spoke.

"Da–a. . .Da–a–a. . .*Dad*!"

I yelled for Roger to come and when he ran in, Taylor just looked at him, like she was thinking, *What. . .?* The next night we were all watching television together and she not only said it again, she yelled it over and over.

"Dad." It was the only word she ever said but she said it. And Taylor was the only proof I ever needed to know that with God all things are possible.

Taylor and Dad during story time

Chapter 22

February 2009 through March 2009

We lived with a wildly fluctuating mixture of anticipation, hope, and dread as we prepared for the rapidly approaching day of surgery. It was scheduled to be performed by Dr. Brown on March 9th. We had no idea what the outcome would be, but Michelle kept reminding me that Taylor was a strong and determined little kid. I knew that. I also knew God was watching over her, watching over all of us.

We battled yet another urinary tract infection and the resulting antibiotics. Fearing that C-Diff would set in, we tried to head it off with probiotics and yogurt. Her weight didn't increase as everyone had hoped it would, due to constipation and the belly pain it caused her. All the while we prayed that her spinal curvature wouldn't reach 100 percent, because then it would be too late for any attempt at surgical repair.

Although I had never tried scrapbooking before, I began putting together scrapbooks for Taylor. It was a lot of fun working on them and after I had finished two, Roger said, "She'll be four in June; how many scrapbooks does she need?"

I said, "Four, I guess!"

We went to a healing service at Melrose Methodist Church a couple of days before the surgery. Everyone prayed for Taylor and our family. Although I was still very nervous, I felt better afterward because

I knew she was already in God's hands and what He decided was the decision I would have accept.

The pulmonologist was still against the spinal surgery, feeling it would lead to disaster. But we had faith God would do what was right for our daughter. We felt that she had already proved to be a miracle many times over. She was a still a fighter and still deserved that tiny last chance.

And she got it!

Dr. Brown had talked to us about going into the surgery room with Taylor until she fell asleep. He said kids don't normally cry if their mom or dad is with them. But the rule was that the parents were instructed not to cry while they were in there. This upset the kids even more. So I practiced over and over. We were in the holding area where patients waited until it was time to go the O.R. Taylor was fine, and Dr. Brown came in dressed in his scrubs for the operating room. Taylor knew right away something wasn't right. She looked scared and looked all around the room, like she was trying to find a way to escape. In came Pastor Bill to pray with us. Taylor was moving all over and wouldn't stay still.

The nurse came in with scrubs for me to put on. When Taylor saw them on me, her eyes had a look of terror in them. We started to walk down the hall. After more than 30 O.R rooms, we finally arrived. They told me to lay her on the operating table which was so thin. It was so cold in there. Taylor was looking around the room in fast jerking motions.

I held her and told her, "Dr. Brown will take good care of you. If we thought you weren't in good hands, we would never do this. Mom and Dad love you more than you know, and we will be waiting for you when you come out."

Her eyes began to close slowly. They said, "She is asleep, mom. You can go now." With my heart breaking, a nurse and I walked out into the hall where I literally fell to my knees, crying my eyes out. The nurse said I did great, not one tear for her to see. But I know she knew this wasn't a good thing.

Connie, Dr. Brown's nurse, took the day off from the office to go into surgery with Taylor. She would come to the waiting room and keep us posted on what was going on and how Taylor was doing. Dr. Brown had guessed the surgery would last around seven or eight hours. Connie had come out a couple of times to let us know Taylor was doing fine and things were going well. Two and a half hours into the surgery, out walked Dr. Brown. Roger, Pastor Bill, Pastor Eileen, her daughter Kathy, Rhonda, Aunt Carolyn, and I all looked at him as if to ask, "What is he doing out here?"

Dr. Brown's glowing face as he came to talk to us said it all. The surgery was a success. Dr. Brown looked so happy when he informed us that he only had to insert one rod instead of two and it had brought the bend in her spine from 95 degrees back to a little less than 30. While the usual blood loss for this type of surgery ran from 800 to 1,000 cc, but Taylor only lost 120 cc. Her vitals remained steady throughout the procedure. And then he asked did you bring the cupcakes? I said I will go home and make you some. To which we all laughed.

We knew she wasn't anywhere near out of danger. In fact, she had a long way to go before we could even think about relaxing a little bit. However, at the moment, she was in the ICU, sedated, and on a ventilator, which we had expected, but managing half of her breathing on her own.

We were not allowed to sleep at the hospital so we went to the Ronald McDonald House to get some rest. I called several times through the night to check on Taylor and she continued to do well. When we got back to the hospital early the next morning, she was on a constant positive airway pressure (CPAP) machine, which supplied continuous gentle pressure to keep her lungs inflated. Eventually, it was turned down to breathe 15 times a minute, with her "breathing over the vent." This meant she was taking breaths on her own without the help of the machine. Since she was on the breathing machine she was still sedated and receiving pain meds. Her eyes were open and she looked at us but, due to all the medications, we weren't sure she really saw us. That, too, was to be expected. I told them I wished I could have had some of that "amnesia" med to block out the previous weeks of worry.

It was Roger's and my wedding anniversary—and sitting there in that hospital with the machines going and medical staff running around, there was nothing more we could have asked for. We even received a card from Taylor for our anniversary. I think I know who sent it, it really meant a lot to us.

Those days at the hospital dragged, often seeming endless, because all we could do was sit and wait. But when it's for a loved one, we try to do whatever it takes to be there for them without complaint. After all the time we'd spent in hospitals with Taylor, I knew by then to take a bag packed with handheld games, puzzle books, and snacks. Friends and family fixed us bags full of goodies and games and stuff to help pass the time—something that was really needed after surgery.

It was a very stressful time because Taylor slept so much and sometimes I just couldn't stop staring at her. We stayed every day for as long as we could keep awake, leaving for the Ronald McDonald House around midnight to get some sleep. The next morning Roger and I were up by around 6:00 a.m. We took our showers and headed back over to the hospital. As early as we got there, Dr. Brown made rounds even earlier and we usually missed him. We were happy that a couple of mornings we got there in time to talk to him. Connie, Dr. Brown's nurse, had told us Dr. Brown had been on cloud nine since Taylor's surgery, because he was so happy with how well things had gone.

Dr. Smith, Taylor's cardiologist, planned on stopping in to check on Taylor at the end of his workdays. He worked at one of the other hospitals, but had patient rights at this hospital and we wanted him to be her cardiologist throughout, because no one knew her like he did. We requested that anything having to do with her heart first be approved by him. And thank the good Lord we did, because he did override some of the changes in her medication the attending cardiologist wanted to make. Right after the surgery, he called to tell Dr. Smith that since Taylor had a heart murmur, she was going to be started on some new drug for it.

Dr. Smith said, "Hold it! Back up the train! She has always had a murmur. She doesn't need that medicine."

It could have caused more damage. We knew it wasn't that they weren't taking good care of her; they just didn't know her like Dr. Smith did.

As the days passed, we were all on edge, waiting for the next step in Taylor's care plan: taking her off the ventilator. The uncertainty had everyone tense, including the medical staff. This had been the biggest worry even before surgery and everyone involved in the procedure was sure we would have negative results.

When Dr. Smith came in, he read her chart and said her numbers looked great.

"I have faith in her," he said. "I want to talk to the attending doctor that will be extubating her."

We went and got her and Dr. Smith told her, "You have to be tough with Taylor. She can do it. I know she can. Don't go easy on her. Make her work. When she knows she has to do it, she will. That's just Taylor. Make her scream if you have to. I can't see her having any problems if you do what I'm telling you."

Everyone was apprehensive right up to the day planned for the extubation. We trusted Dr. Smith because he knew Taylor better than anyone and we hoped the people taking care of her would listen to and

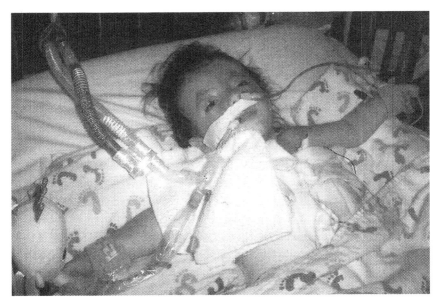

Taylor on the respirator

take the advice he had given. There were seven people gathered in Taylor's room when the time came to take her off the vent. The first thing they did was throw Roger and me out. From outside we could still hear them talking as they prepared.

We heard: "Is this ready? Is this ready? Be ready to put the tube back in. Everybody in place? Go."

Then we didn't hear anything.

Then, all of a sudden, we heard laughing and cheering. When the attending doctor came out of Taylor's room, she had the biggest smile on her face. She told us when the tube was pulled out; Taylor opened her eyes, looked at the people standing over her, and then quickly closed them again. She kept peeking to see if they were still there. The doctor said she did it three or four times, like she was playing a game or waiting for them to stop looking at her. At this point, Taylor was fully awake and not relying on the ventilator to breathe, just supplemental oxygen. Now the attending doctor understood what Taylor was made of. She continued talking to us and said Taylor was a miracle girl with the cutest personality she'd ever seen.

Dr. Smith was absolutely right—Taylor was a tough kid and someone was watching out for her. We all knew who that someone was.

When we were allowed back into the room, Taylor smiled at Roger, but refused to look at me. I felt so bad, but Dr. Brown had warned us she might hold a grudge against the one who turned her over to the medical staff for surgery which, of course, had been *me*. It was two more weeks before that little rascal would even venture a peek at me. It was a very, very long two weeks.

The pulmonologist who had advised against the surgery did not come in to see Taylor, although he had been receiving all her progress reports. We didn't see him after the surgery, but I still sent him a thank-you note for giving the go-ahead and allowing her to have it. We really did appreciate him and didn't hold it against him that he advised against it. He was just doing his job, doing what he felt was medically responsible. He was a good doctor; he just didn't know Taylor well enough to fully understand how tough and resilient our little miracle was.

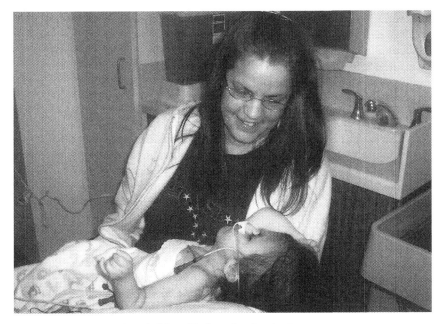

Mom holding Taylor after her back surgery

CHAPTER 23

March 2009 through May 2009

While Taylor was recovering from the spinal surgery, she was scheduled to have a feeding tube surgically inserted her belly two weeks later. It had always been her in nose and down to her stomach, and to the knowledge of her healthcare team, no one had ever had a nasal-gastric (NG) tube that long. It was time for a more a permanent placement. However, the attending physician thought it would be best for Taylor to go home and heal before having that surgery.

Taylor had a lot of visitors in the hospital and they couldn't believe how well she was doing. Dr. Brown checked on his spunky little patient every morning. His nurse, Connie, also checked on her every day. They were such good people. He and Connie informed us that when he went in, Taylor always had the biggest smile for him.

When I told him, "You can quit updating me on the smiles until I get one," he just laughed.

After surgery, Taylor had what looked like a turtle shell on her back. It went all the way around and was open in the front where it tied together. The second night after surgery she pooped all down her legs and up her back. The nurse was sure the doctor wouldn't want the turtle-shell brace removed, so she called him at home.

He laughed and told her, "Take it off and try to clean it the best you can."

It took two nurses and me to get that thing off. The nurse tore all the padding out of the inside and started recreating it. She cut up receiving blankets and got some other cushy stuff and filled it so it would be kind of soft. It took us a couple hours to get Taylor back to resting. When Dr. Brown came in the next morning, he told us we had done a great job. Then the morning came to fit her for her back brace. Don, who made all of Taylor's orthopedic appliances, made it and brought it to her. He had created a very special one just for her because he said, "A special little girl needs a special brace." As a result, Taylor had the first back brace in the world that had a light-up kitty on the front. When she moved it lit up.

❀ ❀ ❀

Taylor touched so many, many people in so many ways and they all appreciated how amazing she was. She brought so many exceptional people into our lives. Some were close to home and we had lived in the same town with them our entire lives, but had never really known them until Taylor came along. I found such good friends and will always be thankful for that.

Our predicted 90-day hospital stay ended up being only nine days. It was so amazing she had done so well. But she had Someone big watching out for her. She always had.

Dr. Brown came in the room and said, "I really don't want to put Taylor out on the floor. There are sick kids out there and that is the last thing she needs. Would you feel comfortable taking her home?"

I said, "Are you comfortable sending her home with us?"

He said, "I wouldn't trust anyone else. It's a miracle that she has done so well. I don't want to take the chance of her picking up a cold or something."

To which I responded, "We would love to take her home!"

So all the necessary paperwork was started. Although I was anxious to get her home, I was also worried about taking care of her once we got there. Her daily care would be more involved than ever. Now she had a steel rod in her back to deal with and I knew it had to hurt. She was

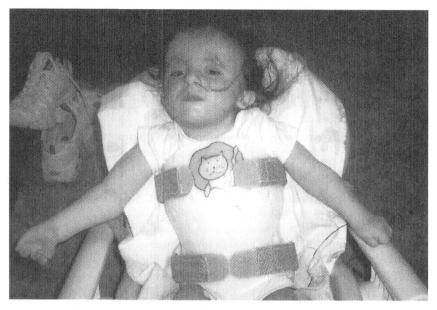

Taylor's specially created back brace with a light-up kitty

to be in the brace 23 hours a day. That would be a chore but we would do our best. She also hadn't had her leg braces on while we were in the hospital and they had to be put back on soon. Keeping her back brace on would be even harder for me this time, because she was very touchy about it, and who could blame her? Questions constantly ran through my mind. *How would we bathe her? What about her pain meds? Was she going to sleep?* These were only a few of my concerns.

When it came time for Taylor's release, Don was putting the finishing touches on her brace at his office. Roger drove over to pick up the brace and we packed our belongings at Ronald McDonald House. Then it was time to go back and get Taylor. While at the hospital, we'd met a Life Flight nurse who flew with our friend Bonnie. He had been observing in the NICU. We found out he only lived about 20 miles from us. He helped Roger carry things to the car. It was the first time that Taylor had been sitting in a seat for a long time and she cried a lot. It had to have been very painful. We tried placing her in her car seat, but because of the brace, she didn't fit very well. I had put blankets under her to cushion her for the long ride, but with the brace on, the belt would hardly reach around her. The blankets were removed, but it was still a tight fit. I promised the nurse I wouldn't put Taylor back in that car seat once we got home. We just needed to get there.

We were finally on our way. I made sure she was given her pain meds right before we left so the ride wouldn't be so rough on her. Before we left, the surgery to move her feeding tube was put on hold to give her time to heal. After we got home, she took regular Tylenol during the day and Tylenol with codeine at night. Dr. Brown didn't prescribe ibuprofen for his back-surgery patients because it can interfere with bone healing. Taylor did very well without it. Life at home went fairly smoothly, with Taylor sleeping well and taking her milk well. She even started back on veggies. It was good to hear her yakking at us again.

On March 24, 2009, we took Taylor back to Dr. Brown for her first post-op check. The incision looked great except for the last quarter inch. It had popped open, probably due to there being pressure put on it by the brace. Fortunately it wasn't infected. X-rays revealed her back was healing just the way Dr. Brown wanted it to. He wanted to see her again in two weeks, to see if the open area improved.

I called Don about the brace and he said to bring her right up and he would fix it. Even though it was a Sunday, he went to his office for us and cut a hole in the back of the brace so nothing would be touching the sore. He also cut the arms out a little since they were rubbing and he put some extra padding behind her neck. Because her head had to be somewhat elevated all the time (because of her reflux), the brace had a tendency to slide up and hit the back of her head.

A week or so after that appointment, I had Michelle look at the open area of Taylor's incision. Just as I thought, Michelle agreed it looked like infection was setting in. She suggested I email a photo of it to Dr. Brown. Since I only had Don's email address, I sent it to him and he forwarded it to Dr. Brown. Later, the phone rang. Dr. Brown wanted us to take Taylor to Toledo the next day so he could decide what to do. He also started her on an antibiotic.

On April 1st, Taylor had additional surgery to clean up the wound and remove dead skin. Then Dr. Brown put in a few stitches to see if it would heal. Then he inserted a wound vac to help promote healing from the inside out. The nurses let me help change the bandages so I could learn about the vac, even though visiting nurses would be coming to the house to take care of it. I was so glad they let me be a part of the procedures.

Through all that, there was good news. While Taylor was in the hospital for that time, she had been completely weaned off the supplemental oxygen. No more hauling that tank around. No more machine running all night. What a day!

When it came time for the stitches to come out, Connie was supposed to remove them because Dr. Brown was on vacation. But when she looked at Taylor's back, she saw something that concerned her, so she sent us down to another office to have Dr. Brown's associate take a look at it. He felt she would be fine until Dr. Brown returned. We went home and went back to see Dr. Brown when he got back from his vacation. He decided to leave the wound vac on for two more weeks.

By then, Dr. Brown was worried that Taylor's back wasn't going to heal.

"Sometimes doctors form an attachment to their patients," he explained to us, "because they want them to do well. I've let Taylor have the wound vac on for about nine weeks and it should've been healed in five weeks, no longer."

Dr. Brown called in a plastic surgeon. He looked at Taylor's back and said, "No way. She's too small. If you graft skin on it the bar will rub underneath the skin and put another hole there. You're going to have to take the rod out."

These were words all of us had been dreading. Dr. Brown tried so hard to avoid it, but it looked like the only way.

Once again, Taylor was scheduled for surgery.

† Chapter 24 †

June 2009 through August 2009

The rod had to be removed. There was no other way. Taylor was in the OR for about one and a half hours for surgical removal of the rod. She did very well. Dr. Brown told us we could take her home after she woke up, but I thought it best to stay at least overnight. It was a good thing we did because she had trouble keeping her oxygen levels up that night. The next day she was better and we went home. We were to return a week later to have the stitches removed. I felt bad every time we had to take her to Toledo because it was a long ride and being buckled in that seat had to be uncomfortable. All I could do was give her pain medicine to help make the trip a little more bearable. She weighed 17 pounds, four ounces. It was the highest her weight had ever been.

In spite of her good weight gain, ever since her last time in the operating room, Taylor couldn't stop throwing up. No matter what we tried, she was constantly sick. Her pediatrician, Dr. Dawson, gave her some medicine, but it didn't help much. I feared the vomiting would cause weight to dramatically fall off her tiny body. Dr. Dawson wanted to know why she was throwing up all the time, so it meant more tests.

The first was a swallowing study. The doctor in X-ray told the technician to put the liquid down Taylor's feeding tube. The technician explained to us that they wanted to see if she could actually swallow it first. The doctor said she couldn't.

Show him what you can do, Taylor, I thought. And she did it. She had an attitude just like me. If you tell me I can't do something, that's all the challenge I've ever needed. The test came back fine, with no swallowing problems.

Taylor turned four on her birthday, June 9, 2009. She was so small, our granddaughter Layla, Michelle's daughter, always referred to Taylor as a baby.

"I'm bigger? Right, Grandma?" Layla would ask.

I answered, "Yes, you're bigger, but Taylor is older."

Well, when Taylor's fourth birthday came around, I knew Layla was starting to figure out that something was different about Taylor.

One day she was so serious when she approached me. She said, "Grandma, Taylor just turned four, right?"

I said, "Yes."

"Well, I'm going to be four in October, right?"

Dad, Taylor and Mom on Taylor's birthday

I said, "Yes."

"Then why can't Taylor walk or talk and play like me?"

This is a smart kid, I thought. I told her, "Well, Taylor has been sick all her life so she can't grow and be strong like you. You can play *with* her, but she really can't play. But she loves you to play *with* her. She loves to laugh at you and she yells a lot."

Layla calmly replied, "And she can yell loud. Right, Grandma?"

"Yes, she can," I agreed.

After that, Layla went on playing, like the conversation never took place.

Layla loved spending the night with us. She played with Taylor even though she really couldn't participate. Layla thought she was helping take care of Taylor and she had made a world of difference. Taylor laughed at her, watched her, and yelled when Layla didn't pay attention to her.

Layla and Taylor—best friends

One night when Layla was staying with us, she was playing on the floor with her teddy bear. It looked like she was operating on the stuffed animal.

Curiosity got the best of me and I finally asked, "What's wrong with your bear?"

Layla said, "Oh, she has to have back surgery. My name is Dr. Brown." She continued, "I took care of Taylor and I'll take care of Teddy. Don't worry, Grandma."

Later, as we were getting ready for bed, I went into Taylor's room to get her pajamas and noticed someone had drawn on the door with a crayon.

Knowing it wasn't Taylor or me, and pretty sure Roger hadn't gone wild with crayons, I asked, "Who was writing on the door?"

Layla said, "*Not me*, Grandma!"

I explained to her no one should write on anything but paper.

She said, "I'll tell whoever did it, okay, Grandma?"

"I would appreciate it," I said.

My Uncle Jim and Aunt Jane Brown called and asked us if we would be interested in doing a benefit for Taylor. They were involved with a big golf outing called the Annual Woodson Memorial Golf Benefit fundraiser. It took place at St. Mike's Golf Course near Defiance, to raise money for families burdened with a lot of medical bills or needing help with something. Uncle Jim brought a man to the house to talk to us about it. He was very nice and was so interested in Taylor. He kept saying, "She's so tiny."

When he and Uncle Jim left, this guy had noticed our roof was in sad shape. So, they asked if they could get the supplies for a new roof. And they did! Gary, Layla's dad, my son Mitchell, my nephew Cody, two of Mitchell's friends, and three of Gary's friends put the new roof on. It looked great and it was wonderful not to have to worry about the sad condition of the shingles anymore. When Uncle Jim saw it, he said they had done a wonderful job.

A lot of people attended the benefit at St. Mike's. Gary played and Roger's cousin came from Columbus to play. Michelle, Layla, Mike,

Stacy, my cousin Diana, Uncle Jim, and Aunt Jane went. It was wonderful to be helped and to help others.

Sometimes I wondered about my mothering skills. Because I was getting older and couldn't remember things as well as I when I was younger, I logged everything I did concerning Taylor. Plus, when she had doctor appointments, they needed to know everything, so I wrote down when I gave meds, how much she ate, if she had a bowel movement, etc. Sometimes, Michelle gave me a hard time about my book full of Taylor's care notes. One day Michelle came in, picked it up to read, and started to laugh.

"What's so funny?" I asked.

She said, "I see Taylor didn't fart today."

It *was* pretty funny.

One day I was having one of "those days." Taylor had been throwing up all day and acted like she didn't feel well. I administered her heart medicine and when I went to write it down, I discovered I had already given it to her two hours before. I was hysterical! I called the hospital and had them page Dr. Smith. His associate called me back right away and told me he was on call for Dr. Smith. I told him what I'd done. I explained I'd been giving Taylor her meds for four years and had never done that before. I was crying. He reassured me.

He said, "She's going to be fine and you are going to be fine. This happens all the time."

I said, "Not to her."

He told me what to watch for and when to take her to the ER. "But I'm sure that won't happen. It's not that big of a dose."

That doctor didn't know me at all, but he was so kind and considerate. I was shaking, but he was right, Taylor was fine.

† CHAPTER 25 †

August 2009 through September 2009

It was August and, at that time of year, Roger loved to go to tractor pulls. I asked Michelle if she would keep Taylor for a day so we could go to one. She never turned me down when it came to Taylor and instantly agreed to watch her. I packed up all the things Taylor would need while she was at Michelle and Gary's the night before and took them over.

Layla asked, "What's Taylor doing? Moving in here?"

I said, "For the day. Is that okay?"

"Yes, I guess," she said.

Roger, his daughter Danielle and her boyfriend, and I went to the tractor pulls. It was a very hot day. My cell phone rang and it was Michelle.

She said, "Mom, I don't want you to worry, but Taylor has a fever."

"How high is it?"

"It's 100.2. . . .I gave her Tylenol. I just wanted you to know and wondered if there's anything else you want me to do."

"Just take some of her clothes off and give her water."

She said, "I already did that."

Michelle's a nurse and she was great with Taylor.

She said, "I have one problem, though."

"What's that?"

She asked, "Are the jealous remarks a common thing at your house?"

"Jealous remarks from Layla?" I asked. "Yes. What is she mad about?"

According to Michelle, Gary had turned a fan on, to stir up the air because it was so hot. She said it was far from Taylor but the cooling effect was for her benefit.

Layla started crying and said, "Taylor gets everything! I get nothing!"

It was said in that little kid way of talking, *"Tayer gets every-sing! I get no-sing."*

I just laughed and told Michelle I was glad it was her turn to hear it that day. It *was* kind of cute, though. I never thought it would be that way between Layla and Taylor, but Taylor had her ways of communicating, too. She let us know if she thought we weren't paying enough attention to her, either. Layla got so mad because Michelle hardly ever called Taylor by her name. She gave her nicknames like Sissy, Tay-Tay, and Tator.

"That's not her name!" Layla would yell. "Call her *Ta-yer!*"

Mom and Taylor

Taylor had been throwing up for weeks. I almost hated feeding times, because I knew what she was going to go through after she ate. I felt so bad. I thought with all that had been tried, they would have found something that helped, but they didn't. No one could put their finger on it. Dr. Dawson decided to send Taylor to a new gastroenterologist on August 26th, to try and find out what was going on. There was *always* something going on with her. And yet—even though she was dealing with constant vomiting and had just gotten over a sinus infection—Taylor still smiled at us.

The new doctor came to our local clinic from Toledo. He was young and very nice and so was his nurse. Taylor had been running a low-grade fever for four days. He decided to put Taylor on C-diff meds for 10 days. After that, she was to have a stool sample checked to make sure it was all clear.

It was also time to go back to Toledo so Dr. Brown could check Taylor's back. It was not a good visit at all. I knew when he walked into the room it wasn't good. He had the saddest look on his face. I was right—we were right back where we had started. Her bend had gone from under 30 degrees to 95 degrees in just that short time. There was no way could she handle having another rod inserted without putting on more weight. It meant she would have to go back on oxygen because of the pressure her spine was putting on her lungs and heart. Dr. Brown set up an appointment with a general surgeon to see about putting the feeding tube in her belly. His thinking was that maybe we could get some more weight on her that way, and then he could put the rod back in. The feeding tube surgery was scheduled for September 29, 2009.

It was Labor Day and Oakwood's homecoming rolled around once again. Michelle and I put the girls in the Kiddy Parade and they won third place. Cheryl said she would help us and Dean volunteered to decorate a wagon. They were so cute. Layla was dressed as a farmer and Taylor was dressed as a pig. Attached to the wagon was a sign that read: OFF TO MARKET. One of my aunts asked Layla, "Why are you selling Taylor?"

Layla looked at her and asked, "How much can I get for her?"

On Monday, we decided to put Taylor and Layla in the big parade with us. We drove the roll-back wrecking truck in the parade with the girls on board.

Taylor had turned four years old in June and Layla would celebrate her fourth birthday in October. They truly made us laugh. We had such a good time. Taylor sat on a horse at the festival and was just adorable.

A couple weeks later Taylor began to run a low-grade fever. It continued for a few days and she was very whiny. Wondering if she was dealing with yet another UTI, I called the clinic to see if her urine could be tested. I requested that Michelle do it. We took her in right away and Michelle used a catheter so we could get the results quickly. It showed the presence of some bacteria. Taylor was started on a round of antibiotics to head a full infection off at the pass. We quickly filled the prescription, went home, and gave her the first dose.

Layla, Michelle, and Taylor in the Oakwood homecoming kiddy parade

It happened that Layla was staying with us that night. We had all gone to bed. Layla was asleep on the little mattress we kept at the foot of our bed for when she slept over. Taylor, however, was very fussy and had a hard time settling down. She finally fell asleep around 3:30 a.m. At 5:20 a.m., her heart monitor went off, reporting a high heart rate. When I picked Taylor up, she was hot to the touch. The thermometer registered 101.5. I immediately called Dr. Smith and had him paged. He returned the call within two minutes.

When I explained what was happening, he said, "We need to get her fever down. She could start having seizures. Do you have Tylenol?"

"Yes."

"Give her a dose and get her into a lukewarm bath," he ordered. "You have to move fast. Call me back if anything changes."

I laid Taylor on the bed with Roger and gave her the Tylenol. I kept the lights low because I didn't want to awaken Layla and Roger if I didn't have to. I left her lying there and hurried to run the bath water. When I went back in, Roger had already started to undress Taylor. I told him to call Michelle because, if we had to go to the hospital, she would need to come get Layla.

I took Taylor to immerse her in the tub. She always slept with her eyes half open, but when I put her in the water, there was absolutely no reaction from her. She should have cried, shivered, or shown some kind of response to being lowered into cool water. There was no movement, no crying. Nothing.

I yelled, "Call the squad!"

Michelle arrived in record time. She took Taylor and held her while Roger and I hurried and got dressed. Layla came down the hall. All the commotion had woken her up.

She said, "Every time I spend the night, Taylor wakes me up!"

Later, I would find humor in what my little granddaughter said. Even in times of emergency, the girls were still in competition with each other for attention.

The squad arrived. Since Taylor's birth, we had continuously kept the local EMS updated on her condition, so that if a 911 call came from our house, they were already apprised of her situation. I was relieved and glad to see my cousin Kirk on the run.

Since Taylor was only clad in a diaper, I'd wrapped her in a blanket. I rode in the back of the squad with her. Kirk was checking her blood pressure and doing other things. During the race to Defiance, where the hospital was located, I tried to get her to respond. Although her eyes were half open, it was as if she was looking right through me. When we arrived at the hospital a breathing tube was put in immediately. Her expression didn't change—it was completely blank. I stayed in the room while they worked on her and put in lines for running meds and blood. I was so scared and a constant prayer was in my heart and on my lips.

Taylor's fever was out of control. When the ER doctor told me they needed to send her by helicopter to Toledo, my heart dropped like a rock. Stunned, I walked out into the hall.

"Kelly," Kirk said, "I called my mom and she's starting the prayer chain."

One of the Life Flight nurses asked if Roger or I would like to ride with Taylor on the helicopter.

"Her mom will," Roger said.

One of the nurses was male, and he spoke sternly to me. "You have to make me a promise," he said. "No matter what happens, you *have* to stay in your seat. *No matter what the emergency.*"

"I will," I promised.

"You look like someone who will keep calm and do what we say," he said.

"I will do whatever it takes," I said. "I don't want her going alone."

They took me to the chopper, showed me where to sit, and gave me a headset. Roger came out, gave me a big hug and a kiss, and told me he would get there as soon as he could. The doctors and nurses hurried out with Taylor on a gurney. They taped her eyes closed. To me, it looked like a bad sign.

We lifted off and were on our way. It was so loud. I could see the medical crew's mouths moving, but couldn't hear anything. One would look at me and give me a thumbs-up and I would give him one. I think it was his way of making sure I was okay. I couldn't keep my eyes off of Taylor. The only time I wasn't watching her was when they were working on her and their bodies blocked my view. Then I just looked out the window. In spite of the noise and confusion, I prayed constantly as we flew through the September dawn, over the patchwork of fields and small towns of northwest Ohio.

CHAPTER 26

September 2009

When we arrived at the ER in Toledo, they worked frantically to insert another breathing tube because they weren't satisfied with the fit of the first one. A central line was started for blood. The entire time, a doctor was peppering me with questions about Taylor. What is Taylor's diagnoses? I said Trisomy 18. What heart condition does she have? A repaired Atrial Ventrecular Septal Defect with a PDA.

I broke in with a question. "If you had to say what shape she is in, what would you say?"

It was a one-word answer: *"Critical."*

The reality hit me with a physical shock that almost brought me to my knees. *What happened? What went wrong? Why didn't I call the doctor sooner? How could I have missed that something was so seriously wrong?*

Although I was frantic to reach Dr. Smith, I wasn't about to leave Taylor alone. Roger arrived a lot more quickly than he would have under normal circumstances, but it still felt like it took him forever to get there. When he arrived, I told him to stay with Taylor because I had to go call Dr. Smith.

"We are at your hospital," I said once I got him on the phone.

"What happened after I talked to you?" he asked.

I began to explain everything that had transpired since I'd made the call to him from home.

"I have to do a couple of things," he said, "and I'll be right there."

When he walked into the ER, my first thought was, *Thank goodness he's here!* Of anyone, he would be able to decipher just what was happening with Taylor. In the meantime, she was transported to ICU, where she was hooked up to a ventilator and every other medical machine imaginable. She wasn't sedated, but was still completely unresponsive. She was being packed in ice. It was then we learned her body temperature had shot up to an unbelievable 108 degrees. The four large zipper-locked plastic bags of ice surrounding her melted within an hour. The doctor told us most adults wouldn't survive a fever of that nature and if Taylor managed to, she would most certainly have brain damage. At times her blood pressure was so low they couldn't get a reading and her pulse so faint it required ultrasound to find it. It took a day and a half to finally bring her fever down. And although some of her numbers looked better, we were told her liver was not functioning and her kidneys had begun to shut down.

We'd arrived in Toledo on a Saturday. It was Sunday and we had no clean clothing, no toothbrushes, nothing. I told Roger we were going to need some things from home. We decided that Monday he would run home, pack our stuff, and take Layla to preschool. All this time, we were still very much involved with Taylor and her caretakers. As two nurses were checking her in, one tended to Taylor while the other asked Roger questions. She asked him how many surgeries Taylor had had since she was born.

He listed them, and then added, "And then there was the time they put in her false teeth."

The nurse stopped writing, stared at him, then looked at me, and said, "Are you serious?"

Roger said, "I'm just kidding you!"

The other nurse said, "She takes everything literally!"

We all laughed. It was a breakthrough moment for us. It broke the ice with the staff. The two nurses laughed and joked with us, and right then, that is what we needed. I didn't want anyone crying in Taylor's room. I didn't want her to know that things were bad and not likely to get better. The director of nursing told the girls not to joke with us because they didn't want our feelings hurt. I explained to her that we had started it and that it was very welcome and much needed break from the stress and worry.

I slipped away from Taylor's room long enough to grab a quick shower. Even though I put dirty clothes back on, it was better than nothing.

When I walked down the hall, back toward Taylor's room, one of the other nurses said teasingly, "It's about time you showered. You need to comb your hair."

I said, "I need Roger's comb."

We laughed. Just those few lighthearted remarks helped me so much. I told her to ask Roger if he had given any thought to showering yet. He told her he would when he got some clean clothes.

Just as Roger was getting ready to leave for home on Monday, without warning Taylor's heart just stopped. Fortunately, a nurse was in the room with us and instantly it filled with doctors and more nurses. CPR was initiated.

One of the doctors said to me, "Come up by her bed and hold her hand. You don't want her to die with strangers."

CPR is the worst thing a parent can ever watch being done to their child. Afterward, I couldn't erase the visions of it out of my memory. It was like a video tape that played over and over and I couldn't turn it off. But the doctor was right—I didn't want my little girl to die surrounded by just strangers.

Dr. Smith had been headed to one of his satellite clinics in Michigan, I asked them to call him and let him know what was going on. He turned around and came back to see Taylor. He told us she had a blood infection, but that her heart looked strong on the monitors. He felt that Taylor, after the tough fight she'd put up all her life, deserved the benefit of another 48 hours, to see what she could do.

"Taylor has come through so much that people didn't think she would," he said. "I don't know if she can make it through this, but she deserves a chance."

He had always been very honest with us. We agreed with him. It was going to be a rough one, but Taylor had always been a tough kid and she needed a chance to see if she could pull through. A lot of doctors looked at her diagnosis and just wrote her off. They couldn't believe she had been with us for four years. But they hadn't seen her fight for her life. And she *did* fight. She fought every single day of her life just to stay alive. One of the doctors at the hospital told us that in 15 years, he had never seen a child with Trisomy 18 survive nearly as long as Taylor.

We put her in God's hands and waited to let Him decide what was best. She was a special child and God gave her to us for a reason. He would decide when she was to go home. We didn't want her to live a meaningless life of pain. She had always been a happy little girl and had blessed us in so many ways.

Six hours after this, she coded again. With CPR, they got her heart going again. Roger had decided against making the trip home. That night Michelle, Gary, Layla, and Mitchell came up to the hospital and brought us everything we needed.

Layla was frightened by Taylor, the tubing, the monitors, and how she looked. Her reaction was to pretend she couldn't see her. I felt so bad for her.

Since the kids had driven our truck up to Toledo, Roger decided to go gas it up while they visited with me. The gas station was just down the street. He'd only been gone about 10 minutes and that's when Taylor's heart stopped again. Once again, I took my place by her side and held her hand. After they got her heart beating again, I called Roger. He was already almost back to the hospital.

It was at this point that I came to the realization that we couldn't keep going on like that. I couldn't stand seeing it and I absolutely didn't want Taylor to continually keep going through it. We were faced with the decision of doing CPR or not. What a choice! Watching it was hard, but saying the words "don't do anything" was even more difficult. It was admitting that there was no hope at all.

We celebrated any little positive change in Taylor's labs. Her kidneys put out a tiny bit and we'd get excited. But, all in all, the news remained dire. Michelle, Gary, Layla, and Mitchell came up every night but one. Roger's daughter Danielle and her boyfriend came up for a couple of visits. Taylor had a lot of visitors and we had an incredible support system. Some people stayed with us, others made repeated trips. Dr. Brown's nurse, Connie, came after work every night to spend time with us at the hospital. She had lost two of her own children and she understood our grief and pain. She became a part of our family and is still a very good friend. We had no way of communicating to her just how much we appreciated her love and support. When Mitchell's girlfriend visited, she brought the scrapbooks I made for Taylor. I was so glad because now the people who had been caring for Taylor could see all her beautiful smiles. They were glad to have a chance to look at them. People who weren't directly taking care of her even came in and asked if they could see the scrapbooks because her nurses were talking about them.

Finally, Roger and I asked all the kids to come and say good-bye to Taylor. We had accepted it was hopeless. Her tiny body was badly swollen and her color so yellow. It was such a sad time, and I knew it was hard on the kids, especially Layla. We had always told her Taylor was a sick little girl. But I also didn't want Layla to get the idea that if she got sick, she would die.

One of her nurses asked if I would like to sleep with Taylor and I told her I would love to. It turned out to be a very important time for me. She had been in a coma since that early morning when her heart monitor had gone off at home. But still I talked to her. The expression on her face will forever be etched in my memory. I believe she heard her mother speaking to her, encouraging her, loving her. That is why I didn't want a lot of crying in her room.

I sang to her. At home the CD player was in the kitchen and we always had music playing. I sang and danced around the room with Taylor in my arms. Sometimes she looked at me as if she thought I was out of my mind. I sat her in her chair while I cooked supper and baked goodies. Sometimes Taylor yelled along to the songs; sometimes she laughed. Now that we were in the hospital, it was my way of letting her know she was with Dad and me. We wanted her to understand that we would stay with her no matter what. I sang, "Jesus loves you, this I know, for the Bible tells me so. . . ." because I wanted her to know God had sent her to us for a special reason.

One of the nuns from the chapel came in one day and asked, "May I sing to Taylor?"

When she finished singing "Jesus Loves Me," I said in Taylor's ear, "Tell her that's not the way my mommy sings it to me."

We laughed and sang it my way.

"That's a much better version," the nun said.

We became very close to the nuns. They spent a lot of time in Taylor's room and were very helpful.

† CHAPTER 27 †

September 2009

Throughout Taylor's life we had always kept everyone up to date on her progress, her up and downs and milestones and breakthroughs, online through Carepages.com. It was a great way of keeping everyone up to date on what was happening. And it allowed our friends and family to support us with their kind and uplifting responses.

Posted September 16, 2009, 1:05 p.m.

Well, I don't know what to update—everything is pretty much the same. Kidneys not working very much, still almost 0, liver shutting down, swelling is pretty bad. I came on here to say, God has given us an angel that we love so much. I can't tell you the many ways she has touched and blessed our lives. And the kids' lives. God will decide when it is time to take Taylor home with him. I have to be honest, she is not doing well. And I wanted to post to ask for prayer and guidance and support. Taylor's organs are damaged from all this trauma and I'm pretty sure I know what we are in store for. And I'm pretty sure so does Roger. I pray God will help us through this terrible time. But in the same sentence, I am saying, "Thank You God for giving us this precious angel to love for more than four years." I would not trade one day or one minute of it. Please remember our family during this time. We will be leaning to God for His comfort and love as always. She is still on no meds to keep her out and she is pretty much unresponsive to us being there. But I'm still singing to her. I know she hears it all.

CAME TO SAY GOOD-BYE. It was a sad time, with Taylor not ᵣₑsponding to anyone. My friend and our pastor were there. When they asked me if I'd held Taylor, I realized I had not. They were right when they said I needed to ask to hold her. Afterward, I was so glad I did. Holding her made me understand what was really going on. She was not going to beat it like the other times.

Taylor was so swollen and jaundiced. When she arrived at the hospital just a few days before, she weighed 18 pounds. Her weight had ballooned up to 27 pounds and it was all fluid because her organs were shutting down.

When Dr. Brown came and visited her he said sadly, "Here's all the weight we needed, but it's the wrong kind of weight."

When I finally held my little girl, she didn't feel familiar to me. She didn't look like Taylor and didn't feel like Taylor. I started to cry.

Roger said, "What's wrong?"

"We are just prolonging what's going to happen, Roger," I said. "Maybe Taylor isn't even really here. Her body is so distorted. We can't keep doing this to her."

Not long after that, Dr. Smith came in.

"We need to talk," he said. "Taylor's numbers are out of this world, in a bad way. I have never seen adults that could survive under these conditions. We have given her 48 hours and things have gotten so much worse. You need to make a decision."

Every doctor who had taken care of her remarked they had never seen such a big fight out of such a little girl. She lived her whole life that way. She was unbelievable. A miracle—I never doubted that.

He said, "I will check with you in the morning." And then he left.

The nurses and doctor who were there that night were all in Taylor's room. The doctor said, "I was talking to my husband about Taylor and he said he knew her. I told him 'No, this little girl isn't from around here.' He said, 'Yes, everyone knows Taylor,' and proceeded to explain everything he knew about Taylor."

The doctor continued, "That is Taylor!"

Her husband added, "Taylor's mom makes the best filled cupcakes!"

I asked the doctor her husband's name and found out he was a resident with Dr. Brown.

"Yes, he does know Taylor!" I said to the doctor.

We kept talking and I told her how Taylor had been born in that hospital and that the doctor who had delivered had said, "Kelly, this is a devastating thing, but these kids just don't survive." I explained how I'd sent him a photo when she was three to let him know she was still here and what all she had gone through. I shared that he took the time to sit down and write back, telling me how much that meant to him.

When the doctor asked what his name was, I told her, "Dr. Wood."

Roger and I were amazed when she said, "He's still here. Would you like to talk to him?"

"I would love to," I said.

When she finished her shift, she found him and told him about us. The next day, Dr. Wood walked into Taylor's room. We were so happy to see him. He told how surprised he was to receive my letter about Taylor and how he never would have guessed she would still be here. He said he felt blessed that I wrote and how thankful he was to have been a part of her life.

He looked at her scrapbooks and said, "She has obviously had a happy life. Those smiles are priceless! I am so glad you asked to have me come up and see her. I wouldn't have missed this for the world."

He told us about a song he wanted us to listen to whenever we could. I gave him a hug and thanked him for taking on our case when no one else would and how thankful we were to have had Taylor in our lives.

Roger and I talked and talked. We, along with Dr. Smith and Dr. Brown, had been so sure she could beat the infection, but it was becoming obvious she couldn't. We were told she had a blood infection—sepsis—and we knew from other people's experience it was a hard thing to survive. They told us any adult with a temperature of 108 degrees usually didn't survive it. But for some reason Taylor had.

I slept with her and sang to her all night long. I told her it was okay to go. The doctors had told us she was fighting hard to stay there with us. So I told her how she would walk and talk and not be sick. And I told her about people up there already who would take great care of her until we came to be with her.

I said to her, "We know you will be in a much better place. And when you get there, look for Grandma Ruthie."

My friend had told me Taylor wouldn't have to look for Grandma because Grandma would be waiting for her. I told Taylor to look for Grandpa Brown, Grandpa Owen, Great Grandma, Cheryl, and Aunt Kathy.

"Aunt Kathy has two babies there you will be playing with," I said.

I tried not to cry when I told her how happy she would be, because I knew our sadness was going to be overwhelming.

"We will miss you more than you will ever know," I whispered.

But I had to let her go because she was suffering. I knew it. I couldn't sleep at all and neither could Roger. It was a decision no one should ever have to make. My mom's machine had to be turned off and my sister's too. And now—Taylor's.

In the morning, the nurses came in and asked if we wanted a paper with Taylor's handprints and footprints. We would add them to Taylor's scrapbook. I was so glad because I had special scrapbook paper for Taylor's prints. The nurses also cut two locks of her hair that will always be precious to me. I had also shown the nurses how to get to Taylor's online care pages so they could read for themselves what a trooper she was.

I wanted Taylor dressed in her own clothes, but it was not going to be easy due to the excess weight. Fortunately, my brother Mike and his wife Stacy had gotten her two outfits made of stretchy material. They had been kind of big on her, but when we put them on her, they fit pretty well. And I wanted her to have lacy socks. So the nurse and I cleaned her up and dressed her and combed her hair. She looked like a doll baby. She *was* a doll baby. I felt like *I* was dying. It was the worst thing I'd ever had to do. *This is the hardest thing I've done yet*, I thought, *but the worst of the worst is yet to come*. I couldn't have been more right.

I was so incredibly sad.

My aunt's husband had told me, "Kelly, you guys have been great parents. God couldn't have chosen any two people better for this task. And if she is meant to live when the machines are shut off, she will breathe on her own."

I could only pray that would happen, but I knew it was a long shot. We had seen miracles with Taylor, but we had never seen Taylor look that sick.

The nurse came in, took the tube out of Taylor's throat, and started unhooking her machines while Roger and I held her. Taylor's heart had always pumped so hard you could see it beat through her clothes. But when I put my hand on her chest, it was so faint, I could barely feel it. My own heart was broken.

Dr. Smith came in with the saddest look on his face. He talked to us about what a fighter she always had been. He told us he was proud to be her doctor.

I asked him to listen to her heartbeat because it felt so faint.

He said, "It's about 35 beats now."

I couldn't stop looking at her and crying. Before he left the room, I asked, "Will you listen to her heart one more time?"

He listened and I knew it was getting harder for him to hear. Dr. Smith always had a certain look when he listened to her heart. Over the four years and three months he took care of Taylor, I had come to know his look of concentration very well.

This time he put the stethoscope down and said, "She's gone. I'm so sorry. I was sure she would beat this."

Dr. Smith was the first to hear Taylor's heartbeat and he was the last. We were so glad he was with us when she passed—not a stranger, someone we didn't know. We thanked him for the great care he had always given Taylor.

† CHAPTER 28 †

September 2009

We spent some time alone with Taylor.

Then a nurse came in and said, "Connie is on the phone. Would one of you like to talk to her?"

I said, "I will."

I told Connie that Taylor was gone.

She asked, "Would you like me to come? If not, it's okay."

I said, "Yes, we need you."

She came right over. We talked with Connie for a while, but then the nurse needed to know what funeral home to call. We told her to call the one right across the street from our house. The people there are so nice and good at their job. They had known about Taylor her entire life and had always known this day could come. As we got ready to leave, I asked the nurse that we had gotten close with to promise me to take good care of Taylor until the man from the funeral home could got there.

"Of course, I will," she reassured me and she gave Roger and me big hugs. "You guys are in my prayers and I am so honored to have been able to take care of Taylor and get to know you."

We felt the same about her.

I can't describe how difficult it was to walk out of that hospital. Each step we took carried us closer to each new wound, like the car with her car seat still in it. I had her diaper bag, and a blanket stained with blood from her central line. I truly didn't know if I was going to make it.

I had already called Mitchell and Michelle from the hospital to let them know about Taylor. I called a few people from the car, including my brothers. The words choked me and I could hardly talk.

We knew we would need something to wear while we were at the funeral home, so we stopped at a shopping center. I had just picked up a few outfits when the saleswoman wanted me to try a different sweater.

I said, "This one is fine."

She said, "Well, this one is. . ."

I interrupted her. "You know, our daughter just passed away a couple hours ago and I really don't care."

She felt so badly and so did I. I didn't mean to come across to her so rudely, but I just wanted to get out of that store and get home.

She said, "I'm so sorry."

I said, "No, I am the one that's sorry."

We left the store. I felt bad about the store clerk. I cried, feeling bad about everything, Taylor, me, Roger, the kids—everyone who had played a role in Taylor's life—and that was a lot of people. On the way home I wondered how I could ever be motivated again without her. She was what I had done for the last four years and three months. My life had totally centered on Taylor's as I tried to provide the best care and all the love she needed. I knew there had been times the kids felt like we weren't there for them. It had been especially difficult for Danielle, Roger's daughter. It was hardest for her because she was young and played sports and thought we just didn't want to go to her games. I hoped someday she would understand why her Dad so often went to her events by himself and I stayed home with Taylor. I did make a few games, but it had not been easy to get there. Michelle and Mitchell were grown, but it was hard for Michelle sometimes, too. She would call and want for us to go shopping and there were so many times we couldn't. We could no longer do the things together we used to. But I also knew she understood how important it was to keep Taylor at home. She loved Taylor with all her heart, but I was sure she and the others felt neglected sometimes. I just hoped and prayed they understood.

The next morning, I wrote the update on the care page.

Posted September 19, 2009, 7:21 a.m.

I am truly heartbroken to write this update today. Today for those of you who don't know, Taylor lost her battle with the infection and gained her wings. She was always an angel but is truly an angel now. God called her home—the fight was too big for her. Taylor fought the hardest we've ever seen her fight. I can't tell you how many times we heard this week what an angel she was, which we already know. I have said from day one God has given her to us for a reason, and her job here must be done. Is it easy to accept? Absolutely not. But I know deep down she is in a better place. I told her yesterday she will be able to talk, walk, play, and sing. And we would miss her more then she would ever know.

We would like to thank you all for the years of prayers for Taylor. You have all been so committed to these pages, to watch her progress and struggles, and we can't say how much we appreciate it. It has been so encouraging to read your messages and get your phone calls and cards. These pages have been a blessing, and so have you. Please pray for our family during this heartbreaking time. Thank you for always being there for us. God, I'm sure, has Taylor on His knee, telling her how much He loves her, and how proud He is of her.

I KNEW THE NEXT FEW DAYS WOULD be the hardest I'd ever had to endure. I had no idea how I would handle it. My mind just would not shut down. It ran relentlessly as I worried first about this, then about that, all the details and decisions we would be forced to make, no matter where we were emotionally. As we drove home, I kept looking over at Roger, whose face was completely blank. It stayed that way all the way home.

In addition, I was very concerned about how Layla was going to handle it all. She and Taylor had been the best of buddies for almost four years.

I called Michelle and Mitchell to tell them we had arrived home. They had always been Taylor's biggest supporters. They came right over and there she was—Layla.

She came right to me, gave me a big hug and kiss, and asked, "Grandma, did Taylor pass away?"

"Yes, she did," I said.

"Well, where is she?"

I said, "She went to heaven to live with Jesus."

"Because she was so sick and only Jesus can take care of her and make her better, right Grandma?" Layla asked.

I simply said, "Yes."

It was all so confusing for her. I fervently hoped that I'd told her the right thing and hoped she could understand. But she was such a little girl and we were talking about her best friend.

Not long after the kids came to the house, one of the funeral directors called. "Kelly, I have Taylor back."

I said, "I have a question. Is there anything you can do about all of the swelling?"

He said, "Kelly, I have already taken care of that. She looks like your precious Taylor."

I said, "Thank you so much. I was worried about that."

He said, "She looks beautiful."

I called Danielle's mom to tell her Roger wanted to come and tell Danielle about Taylor. I don't really know how it went between Roger and his daughter. I stayed home to get Taylor's things ready for the next day. We bought her a dress, tights, and shoes on the way home from the hospital. We knew there was no way any of her clothes would fit her since she had put on so much extra weight due to the fluid.

We met with the funeral director the next day. We needed to take Taylor's clothes, write the obituary, and make the funeral arrangements. As we trudged through each step, each task that was required of us, I couldn't believe it was happening. Even though we tried, when the time came, we realized there was no way we could have ever prepared ourselves for Taylor's death.

Immediately people started bringing to the house food, paper plates, and pop. Anything we were going to need over the next few days was provided. The phone rang constantly, so Michelle took care of all the calls.

All the while, Layla followed me around like a little lost puppy, peppering me with endless questions.

"Did Taylor cry when she died?"

I said, "She just went to sleep."

She continued, "Were you holding her?"

"Yes, Papaw and I both held her."

"Did you cry?"

I couldn't imagine what it was like being a little kid and losing my best friend. It was September and Layla would turn four years old in October. I couldn't believe the questions she asked. I tried to answer them to the best of my ability and hoped what I told her wouldn't damage her for life.

† Chapter 29 †

September 2009

My Grandma Ocie always told me, "It hurts when you lose a loved one, like a parent, a sibling, or your spouse, but there is no hurt like losing a child, no matter what their age." She had lost five out of her seven children, so she would know. I always told her I hoped I never had to know that feeling. But some things we cannot change, no matter how hard we try.

And she was right. I felt so empty and lost, like I didn't know what to do next. But I would soon tell myself, *I can't just give up*. Although no one believed Taylor would survive more than a day, it was a gift to have had her with us for over four years. I knew I had to go on. I had a family who needed me.

While I felt so blessed to have had Taylor for as long as I did, I found myself walking around adrift. I didn't know what to do. Taylor's multiple issues required a tight schedule from the very beginning. It had been crucial that everything be done at certain times in order to fit in all that her care required: meds, baths, appointments, therapy, plus all the little everyday tasks. No longer needing to do those things turned out to be one of the most trying aspects of the days, weeks, and months that followed. It was so ingrained in me, that I automatically kept thinking: *Time for Taylor's meds*, or *time for this*, or *time for that*.

Her bed had always been in our room because we were afraid to have her too far away, especially with the heart monitor and oxygen alarms. The mornings following her death, looking at that empty crib was almost more than I could take.

Although it would have been easiest to give myself over to the feelings of emptiness and loss, I told myself I just couldn't give up.

My brother Mike was on his way from Alabama, but wouldn't arrive until evening. His wife Stacy stayed home with their kids. Their daughter Abbie was having a really hard time dealing with Taylor dying and they had decided it might be best to keep her at home. I told them whatever they decided was fine with me. I knew it was going to be hard, no matter what. Mike and Stacy had always treated Taylor like she was one of their own. They were the ones who were to take Taylor if anything ever happened to Roger and me.

My brother Tim was going to come from Alaska, but when I talked to him, I realized how much it would cost for a last minute ticket. I told him he didn't need to come, that it would mean a lot to me if he just checked from time to time to see how I was doing. Stacy and Tim called every day. It meant so much.

The day came to go to the funeral home. I felt sick. I was in the bathroom brushing my teeth when Layla came in and asked to brush her teeth. I told her she could when I was done.

In response she said, "Just let me use Taylor's toothbrush. She won't be using it anymore."

I about fell over. But there was a story behind her remark. For a year, Taylor and Layla both had Dora the Explorer toothbrushes, each in a different color.

Layla always said, "Let me use Taylor's; she can use mine."

I always told her the same thing: "No, we always use our own."

On the day of the funeral, she didn't argue. She used her own. It didn't end there, however. For two weeks after Taylor died, Layla persisted.

"Taylor's not coming back. Why can't I have her toothbrush?"

I didn't know what to do about it. She wouldn't let it go. I finally hid Taylor's toothbrush.

A couple weeks later, here came Layla again. She said, "Grandma, I think Taylor took that toothbrush to heaven with her."

I said, "I bet she did."

That was the last time we talked about the toothbrush.

We arrived at the funeral home. We walked in the doors. Layla walked between Michelle and me, holding our hands. Suddenly a look of shock flooded her face.

"What is Taylor doing here?" she yelled.

I looked at Michelle and I said, "Oh my gosh! I told her Taylor went to heaven to live with Jesus."

Layla was beside herself as she struggled to comprehend Taylor's death.

She kept saying, "Is she real? What is she doing here? Well, why is she here?"

We took her up to the casket and she put out her hand and touched Taylor's arm and said: "It is Taylor. She's real. Why is she here?"

I took her to a chair, sat her on my lap, and said, "Jesus won't be able to pick her up for a couple days."

"Because He's busy?"

I said, "Yes, but He will come and get her soon."

She then said, "Grandma, don't leave her here by herself. She will be so scared. She doesn't like to be by herself."

I explained the situation to the woman working at the funeral home. She kindly agreed to tell Layla, if she asked, that she would be staying with Taylor so she wouldn't be alone.

Taylor looked adorable. . .so cute. . .as if she could just get up and walk away. I don't know how many times I heard, *"She looks healthier than she ever did."* She wore the baby ring my friend Val had gotten her before she was born. At four years old, it was still too big for her. It is difficult to describe just how small Taylor was. I bought her a dress with pink ballerina shoes on it.

I made a remark to one of my friends, "I know she never walked, but they are so cute."

She replied, "She's walking now. It's perfect. She looks like a doll baby."

Many, many people came to the funeral home during visitation. It was unbelievable the people our little daughter had touched. Roger and I didn't sit down or take a break all night, because the line of people paying their respects was endless. We didn't want to take bathroom breaks for fear of missing someone. An early autumn thunderstorm rumbled through the area and suddenly the lights went out. The funeral home staff brought out candles and placed them around Taylor's casket so people could still go through the line and see her.

It was amazing. Visitation was two nights, nonstop, of people showing us how much they cared. Taylor really left her mark, gracing people all over the United States. We received cards from across the country, some from people who had heard about her from relatives or friends and who had prayed for her, some from those we'd met at the hospitals in Michigan and Toledo. I saw nurses, doctors, family, friends, and people I had worked with and people who worked with Roger. *This little girl was definitely sent here for a purpose*, I thought. *I believe she filled the order.* God sent her to us for a reason and from the show of friendship, kindness, and sympathy before us, she had completed her assignment and done it well. It was all so touching. My brother Mike commented later that he didn't know his sister knew so many people.

† Chapter 30 †

September 2009

The most difficult day—the day of the funeral—was fast approaching. We went to the church for the service. The sanctuary was full of people!

We had an hour of visitation before the service. When I looked up and saw Dr. Dawson and his nurse standing there, I couldn't help but cry. I hugged him and told him how much we appreciated the great care he'd given Taylor and how much it meant to us that he put her needs first, thinking of ways to ease our care for her. He did a lot of doctoring over the phone, setting up lab work so we wouldn't have to wait, and even allowed me to play doctor at times. It touched our hearts deeply that he had come.

He said, "I am so glad to have helped, and you made it easy to let you doctor her. You were pretty good at knowing what was going on and what to do with her."

It was just about time for the service to start when I saw Connie, Dr. Brown's nurse, walk in. She'd driven down from Michigan to get there. Seeing her was a real surprise and I was so glad she came.

We had just taken our seats when the side door of the church opened and I saw a wheelchair. I couldn't believe it, but there he was, my cousin Norm. He had ALS, but despite how ill he was, he and his wife Peg, one of my best friends, had made the trip from Tennessee. My cousin Doug had driven up with them from Tennessee so they could be there with us.

I was so touched by all the people who gathered there with us. I was struck by the realization of just how many people cared about us and had taken the time and effort to be there for us. I was humbled and awed, seeing all the family members and friends who had come from our surrounding communities.

I had asked my cousin Diana to read a poem I'd gotten from Mitchell's girlfriend. It fit so well. The words described Taylor perfectly and will always be special to me.

God Sent an Angel to Earth

God sent an angel to the earth, the sweetest angel too,
and for such a tiny little thing, she had so much to do.
She knew she did not have much time upon this earth to stay,
so she got started right away.
Her eyes were bright and sparkly, she took in every turn.
She did not miss a single thing, because Taylor came to learn!
God sent her here to touch the hearts of those he could not reach.
She taught them courage, strength, and faith, because Taylor came to teach.
Her tiny body was so full of God above,
you felt it when you held her, because Taylor came to love.
In four short years she managed what many never will.
When she went home to Jesus, her purpose was fulfilled.
She learned and taught, loved and played, she learned her lessons well.
I know He was so proud of her when she went home to dwell.
But when I miss her OH-SO-MUCH, I can almost hear Him say,
"Please understand, her work was done.
Taylor did not come to stay."

After the service, Roger's and my churches went together and provided a luncheon. Once again, we were overwhelmed. It was more than I could've expected. We spent the day visiting with the people Taylor touched in so many wonderful ways. It was so nice that people who had played such important roles in Taylor's life were able to finally meet others who were so special to her, too. We stayed at the church until late in the evening.

When Taylor was in the hospital the last week of her life, Taylor's teachers, Deedi and Beth, had traveled up to see us. While they were there, they met Connie, Dr. Brown's nurse. The connection was immediate; it was as if they had always known each other. After the funeral, Connie rode to the cemetery with Deedi, Beth, and Angie, Taylor's physical therapist. They bonded in friendship because of Taylor. One of the many wonders of Taylor was the way she brought such good friends into our lives.

Although we were physically and emotionally exhausted, when it was finally time to go home, it was hard to leave the warmth, kindness, and comfort of the church. When we arrived home, the kids were all there waiting for us, but someone was missing. *Taylor.*

The kids went home late that night and Danielle went back home to her mother's. Then it was the time I may have dreaded most. Once again, it was just Roger and me. The house where Taylor's existence had shaped our days and nights was suddenly and incredibly quiet. It had been a very busy, happy home as we fed Taylor, administered her meds, gave her baths, played with her. . . and loved her. Before that night, I never knew that the simple lack of sound and activity could be painful.

I wondered, *How will we ever get through this?*

CHAPTER 31

September 2009

We said a lot of prayers during those first days, asking God to provide the strength we needed to keep putting one foot in front of the other. Getting through each day without Taylor took more energy than it had ever taken on her worst day.

My brother Mike stayed on for a couple days after Taylor's funeral. I have to admit, I didn't want to say good-bye to him.

I told him, "I hate for you to leave, but I know you have a family and I know how much they need you."

When he offered to stay another day, I said, "I'm okay."

So, he left that day. However, I have the best brothers. They called me at least once a week for months after Taylor's death. I hope they know how much it meant to me. My friend Kim lives in South Carolina and had always called to check on Taylor. She continued to call after Taylor passed away, just to talk, just to listen. I was so thankful for her.

Most people are very uncomfortable hearing about a child who has died. They did not want to talk to me about Taylor. Even if I was the one who brought up her name, suddenly they had to go. They weren't being mean or rude. I understood they didn't know what to say, or they worried about saying the wrong thing, or that I might cry. Grieving parents *need* to talk about their children. It may have been months or even years, but we are still working through our sadness and loss. It takes so long and talking is one way of working through it. Each time I hear Taylor's name on someone else's lips, it is a joy to know she mattered to them. To this day, when I know someone will talk to me about Taylor, I will talk.

We didn't have life insurance on Taylor. We learned when Taylor was born that kids born with heart defects were uninsurable. As a result, we had no idea how we were going to pay for her funeral. The funeral director told us they would work with us and suggested we have the memorials go toward funeral costs. The generosity of people was once again overwhelming. We were allowed to use the money from the P. Buckley Moss Foundation Trees of Life fundraiser. It was to go for the purchase of special equipment for Taylor. We never had a chance to purchase it. The group that sponsored the golf benefit at St. Mike's also contributed.

With the support of our family, friends, neighbors, and those organizations, we were able to cover the cost of Taylor's funeral and purchase her headstone. I have learned to never think people don't care, because they do. Their willingness to come to our aid at such a time was yet another blessing!

About three weeks after the funeral, Taylor's baby bed was still in our room. I had been having dreams about her death. I never saw her face, but I knew that's what I was dreaming about. I began to think I should take down the bed, because waking up every morning to the sight of an empty crib was more than I could stand. Deedi said she would help me take it down and Roger said he would help whenever I was ready. One day, and I still don't know what came over me, I went in and just started taking it down. I wondered briefly how Layla would take it.

The next day she came over. When she discovered the bed was gone, she was so upset she started yelling.

"Why did you take Taylor's bed away? What did you do with all the toys? Where is all the stuff?"

I had no idea she would react so strongly. I felt terrible. I promised her I wouldn't get rid of anything.

I tried to explain to her. "Taylor won't be using the bed and we'll save everything for later."

Michelle said, "Mom, I am so sorry she keeps saying things to you."

"If there's anyone who will miss Taylor as much as us, it's Layla. I would rather that she ask than keep it inside," I said.

It wasn't easy for me to handle Layla's endless questions about Taylor. In fact, I really struggled with some of her remarks. But I reminded myself that she was just a little kid. I recalled what my mom used to say: "You can't talk to a more honest person in the world than a kid. They will give it to you straight and from the heart." She was so right.

One day a toothpaste commercial came on and just out of the blue Layla said, "Grandma, I bet Taylor has the whitest teeth in heaven. Don't you think so?"

I laughed and said, "I bet she does."

Layla had just started preschool the month before. Taylor started the same time, but her sessions were at our house and just once a week. A part of Taylor's and my daily schedule was to take Layla to school and pick her up. They always rode in their car seats next to each other and I wondered if that was why Layla talked about Taylor a lot when we were in the car.

We would be driving down the road and Layla would say, "I really miss Taylor. Don't you, Grandma?"

"I sure do."

After Taylor's death, we had been advised not to be in a hurry to put Taylor's things away or get rid of anything until we felt we were ready. So Taylor's car seat remained in the car for some time.

One day, Layla asked, "When are you going to take Taylor's car seat out? I don't have a lot of room back here."

I said, "Well, her seat was in here long before yours and we've never had a problem before."

That night as I was telling Roger about our little conversation from that afternoon, I said, "I always had Taylor's seat in the middle of the backseat. She's not riding there so I need to move Layla's over to the middle."

I went right out and took Taylor's car seat out and moved Layla's over to the middle.

When I picked her up the next day, she stretched her arms out wide and said, "This is what I'm talking about."

I turned around, looked at her, and just laughed. Layla is so funny. I couldn't stop myself from laughing at some of her comments. Our granddaughter has always kept life interesting.

CHAPTER 32

October 2009

Roger and I were affected by Taylor's passing away very differently. He was angry at the loss of his daughter, while I viewed it as though she had been a temporary gift. She wasn't supposed to be here one day and we had her for four years, three months, and nine days. To me, it was the biggest miracle of all! Two days before Taylor died, a baby was born at the hospital, also with Trisomy 18. Although that baby actually had fewer problems than Taylor had, he passed away at the age of three months. Why did Taylor live to be four years old? I believe it was God, prayers, and the fact that Taylor was a fighter. Doctors had told us that she knew she was loved and it helped fuel her fight. I can't imagine not giving her a chance. And she grabbed tight onto every chance that was thrown at her. The more that went wrong, the harder she fought.

Roger wasn't the same after Taylor's death. One day he mentioned I had too much stuff on the bulletin board.

I said, "Roger, it's mine and I painted it. It has my name on it. Do you want me to make you one?"

He said, "No, just forget it. If you don't want to see what you've got up there, I guess it's your business."

I said, "I know what's up there."

Right before Taylor died, our refrigerator broke. Because it wasn't repairable, we had to buy a new one. I'd always wanted a black fridge, so that's what I chose.

One day Roger said, "I buy you a new fridge and you cover it up with a bunch of pictures."

I said, "Roger, those pictures were on my old fridge. Do you want me to take them down?"

"No, just forget it."

As for being there for us, he always was. But it wasn't my Roger. He was really going through a rough time about Taylor. I was at the clinic one day and talked with Dr. Smith. He asked how Roger was doing.

I said, "Not good. He is having a bad time. I think he's mad, because Taylor seemed to be getting through a lot of the bad stuff and she couldn't beat this. And I think he wonders why."

Dr. Smith said, "Kelly, it could take up to two years for him to be able to even talk about it.

Part of the problem was Roger's schedule. He was hardly ever home. He'd had to work two jobs so I could stay home and take care of Taylor. I think this really bothered him, that he missed out on being home with us. If he hadn't worked that much and I'd had to work, too, she probably wouldn't have been with us for four years. Staying home with her allowed us to basically isolate her and prevent her from being dragged out and around other sick kids.

I felt so bad as I remembered the night Roger came home from the shop, ate, and then had to leave right away for his third-shift job. Taylor always got a kiss from him, and then as he walked away, she watched him until she couldn't see him anymore.

When he turned the corner by the kitchen on his way out, I said to her, "Who was that man?"

I was just kidding, but I think it really hit him hard.

In the months after Taylor died, we both struggled with our grief in different ways. One day Roger called home as I was listening to a recording we have of her talking and yelling.

He asked, "What are you doing?"

"Listening to Taylor's voice," I said.

Every year when I baked holiday goodies, Taylor was always in the kitchen with me. The first Christmas, just a few months after her death, was incredibly sad for me. After spending the day baking, I told Roger that it had been a rough day.

He asked, "Why?"

"Baking was so lonely today."

He said, "I'm sorry."

Roger became very quiet and reserved. Dr. Smith advised me to have patience because it would take time.

Jon and Becky Jo, very good friends of ours, put Taylor and Layla's videos on DVDs and made a bunch of copies for us. I didn't want to upset him, so I watched them when Roger wasn't home. I made it my time and sat and watched them. Sometimes I laughed; sometimes I cried. One day as I was watching the movies, Mitchell came in. I thought he would turn around and walk out, but he sat and watched it with me and even laughed at times.

Then he asked, "Mom, how old was Taylor there?"

I said, "Four or five months old."

He said, "Boy, she learned to ignore you at an early age!"

He was right! If we got the video camera out Taylor looked anywhere but at the person behind the camera. Sometimes she would quickly glance back to see if I was still there. If I was, she'd look away. It was so funny.

When my friend, Kim, was home for a visit, she invited Roger and me over to her parents' home.

When we got there, Kim said, "I was so afraid to see you. I couldn't imagine you without Taylor. I thought you would look awful, but it's not like that at all! You look good and I'm so glad to see you. It is sad you don't have Taylor, but we know she's in a better place. And, I know you; you will always keep her memory alive."

"Yes I will. That won't be a problem." I was so glad to see my dear friend and share stories about Taylor with her.

Taylor was a very precious angel, and when people met her, they never forgot her. The woman who took Taylor's picture at Wal-Mart was always so patient and thought Taylor was such a miracle. I always requested her because she was great with Taylor. Even now when we go in, she has a hug for me and tells me how much she loved taking Taylor's photos. It wasn't always easy. Taylor was not one to smile on cue. I got on the floor in front of her and Roger held the back of her dress in a sitting position. Then I took her monkey and played with her to get her to smile. That's why in a lot of her pictures she's looking to the side or down. People, like that photographer, don't know how much it means to others when they go a little bit out of their way to show how much they care.

Roger went on a wrecker run one day and when he got back home, he had a big framed P. Buckley Moss print with him.

I asked, "Where did you get that picture?"

He said, "The run I went on. The woman who won the first prize for Taylor's Trees of Life benefit raffle won this, and she asked me to give it to you. She thought you would like to have it."

That meant so much. I will always cherish that print and the fact she gave it to me in memory of Taylor.

Michelle's friend at work lost her dad. She and her brother were going to start attending grief meetings. She asked Michelle if Roger and I would be interested in joining them. I told her we would. So we started going, and once again, we met the nicest people. They were people who had been through really the same thing, loss. It was a place where Roger would let down and talk about Taylor, which was great. The meetings helped me a lot, too. Meeting with other bereaved people helped me understand unexpected things I'd been experiencing.

Until then, I had no idea why some days I would wake up, and even before my feet hit the floor, be crying and continue to cry all day. I asked myself, *Why am I crying?* It didn't feel like I was crying about Taylor, but I learned it was part of my grieving process. I came to understand that the way Roger was acting was totally normal. At our last session, one of the group members told me he had seen a huge difference in Roger. I had too, but at that point, he still had a way to go.

The people in the group had never met Taylor and our group had finished meeting long before, but on Taylor's birthday the next June, we received cards from the couples telling us they knew it would be a hard day. I didn't even know they knew when her birthday was. They wanted us to know they were praying for and thinking of us. Those cards meant so much. Two years after her death, Taylor is still working in our lives. She brings us good friends and good people with whom to share our feelings. I know that's her work.

Chapter 33

November 2009

Just a few days before Thanksgiving, Roger informed me that he had a rash and that it had been hurting awhile. So I asked Michelle to stop over and look at it. As soon as she saw it, she told him he had shingles. She talked to Roger's doctor and he sent a prescription home with her so Roger could get started on it. The doctor took this quick action because he knew if Roger didn't start the medicine, the shingles would be really bad by the time he could see Roger.

When we went to the appointment, the doctor looked at the rash and said, "Boy, do you have shingles!" Then he added, "These are usually brought on by stress, you know?"

It was easy to understand that! Our daughter had just died, and during all this, Roger's daughter Danielle had begun having seizures. A lesion was discovered on her brain and surgery was scheduled for its removal in hopes it would help control the seizures. She did well, but at that time, Roger's nerves were on overload. It took a long time for him to get over shingles.

I kept telling him, "You should talk more about what you're feeling. I talk about how I feel all the time and you don't see me with shingles."

I didn't want to sound mean; I just wanted him to know letting it out was so much better than keeping it in.

Layla came up with another gem! She was always making up sweet little songs about Taylor.

She often asked, "Do you want to hear a song about memories of Taylor?"

I never want her to stop talking about Taylor.

A couple months after Taylor died I got a phone call from Ron, my cousin Diana's husband. There was never a time that he didn't acknowledge Taylor or missed a chance to hold her. He loved her.

He said, "I didn't know if I should tell you this, but Diana said I should." He continued, "I had a dream last week about Taylor. It seemed so real that when I woke up, I kept reminding myself it was just a dream." He went on to say he saw Taylor riding on someone's shoulders. "I don't know whose shoulders they were, but Taylor's back was straight as a pencil, her hair was blowing in the breeze, and she was laughing and talking." He said to me, "Kelly, she's okay."

His dream was so real, I cried. I had not had one dream about Taylor at that point, so I told him, "If you ever have any more dreams, please call and tell me. I can't tell you how much this meant to me."

I told our pastor about Ron's dream and asked why I never dreamed about Taylor.

She said, "Because you aren't ready. This is how God works, through other people."

Roger's sister Terry sent us a letter about a dream she had. In it she related that everything was so beautiful, and Taylor was running and playing and sitting on Jesus' knee and she was telling Him it was so hard to leave us.

Taylor never walked or talked or sat up here on Earth. The visions of her being able to do all those things with childlike abandon meant the world to me. Because of Ron and Terry, I can imagine Taylor laughing, running, and playing with the other kids. She is in the best place, and with people who love her and will take care of her. I'm still waiting, but I still haven't had any dreams about Taylor.

One of Taylor's doctors had suggested to us that, although it wasn't documented anywhere, Taylor might have died from the H1N1 virus. He believed that based on how fast she got so bad, the way her temperature was so high, and the way things happened with her organs and such. Somehow that knowledge made me feel better. We were still reeling from losing her, but at least the Trisomy 18 hadn't had the final triumph. We'd been told since I was 15 weeks pregnant that she wouldn't survive because of the Trisomy 18. So if that doctor is right, and in my mind he is, she beat the Trisomy 18. That makes us even more proud of her. We knew she was a fighter and a gift from God. Through her we learned to never stop believing and to have faith in God.

Taylor was an extraordinary kid, and tough. Since the day she was born, she was a fighter. Any kid who lived in pain all the time and yet always had a smile on her face had to be special. Anyone who took an interest in Taylor found out that it was so easy to become attached to her. I feel sorry for the people, and they are only a handful, who didn't want anything to do with her. They are the ones who missed out getting to know a special little girl.

In December, we went to a holiday remembrance program held by the funeral home. We were given a glass angel ornament with Taylor's date of birth and date of death on it. The guest speaker told the story of when her family lost a loved one, they lit a candle on holidays in remembrance. When I went home, I decided to make our own arrangement with a candle to light for Taylor at Christmas. It felt good to be creating something pretty. When it was finished, we gathered around it with the kids to light the candle the first time. Then I took the arrangement to my family's Christmas gathering. I asked my cousin Sue to read a little book in memory of Taylor. Then we lit the candle in memory of all the family members who had gone on before us. I was glad we did it, because it wasn't just me who appreciated it. I hoped it would become a family tradition.

† CHAPTER 34 †

June 2010

In June 2010, I posted on my Facebook page, *Today would be Taylor's 5th birthday and Layla will spending the day with me. And we are having a fun day.*

I said to Layla, "At 1:17 p.m., we will light Taylor's candle, because that was the time she was born. And we will sing 'Happy Birthday' to her."

All morning she kept asking, "Is it 1:17? Is it 1:17? Is it 1:17?"

Later I told Michelle I would never tell Layla a specific time again. Layla was sitting on my lap as I was talking on the telephone to my friend and Taylor's teacher, Deedi, as I was reading off the Facebook comments that had come in response to my post.

I read aloud one of my cousin's posts: *"Maybe God got Taylor a pony for her birthday."*

Layla jerked around, looked back at me, and shouted, *"What!* Taylor got a pony for her birthday?" She said, "I'm going right up to heaven and getting me a pony."

I said, "She didn't say she *did* get one. She said *maybe.*"

Layla said, "Well, I'm going there to find out."

Deedi and I laughed so hard. The things Layla says would make anyone laugh. That night I told Michelle to ask Layla what Taylor got for her birthday.

Later Michelle said, "You're never going to believe this. She got either a pony, a carousel, or a unicorn. Can you believe that?"

Michelle also told me Layla was ticked.

Layla may have been disgruntled over Taylor's pony in heaven, but it was obvious she missed her dear little friend.

We would be driving down the road and she would say, "I miss Taylor."

"Me too," I'd reply.

And Roger added, "Me three."

She talked about Taylor and the things we used to do together. I used to wonder why Michelle and I were pregnant with the girls at the same time. Now I knew. God knew we would need Layla to help us along the way as we traveled that seemingly endless road of grief.

Later on that day of Taylor's fifth birthday, my two cousins, Lisa and Patti, came and took me to the cemetery. They brought two sparkly, shiny balloons and we put them on Taylor's grave. That meant a lot to me. Rhonda came to the house and had a birthday gift for Taylor. Every year on Taylor's birthday, she brought her a ceramic number—the number of Taylor's age that year. The year before, when she went to purchase Taylor's birthday number, she found the store was going out of business, so she went ahead and bought one for the next year. She gave it to me on Taylor's birthday so I could put it on her shelf with the rest. It gave me such happiness to put that little number up on shelf with the others.

※ ※ ※

I had an idea and was determined to see it become reality.

When Taylor died, Jeannie, Roger's niece, and her family gave us a book called *Mommy, Please Don't Cry: There are No Tears in Heaven.* Well, I refused to touch that book for about three months, thinking, *If it's called* Mommy, Please Don't Cry, *I'm sure I will.* Finally, one night I picked it up and began to read. The words on the first page were: "Mommy, please don't cry; a beautiful angel carried me here." I just burst out crying and continued to cry at every page, all the way through the book. Every night after that, I read that book. It was as if Taylor herself was telling the story. Then one night I decided to read it to Layla and she picked right up on it.

She said, "Grandma, Taylor is telling us she's okay, right?"

"That's right," I said.

With that, it became a very popular book at our house. Layla and I read it together every time she spent the night.

I wanted to buy copies of that book to donate to the hospital in memory of Taylor.

I wanted families experiencing the death of a child to receive one. It had helped Layla and me so much—certainly it could help others.

I found that taking positive action in Taylor's name was healing. An activity that helped me deal with my sadness was to collect pop tabs for Ronald McDonald House. The tabs are recycled and the proceeds help pay their bills, which helps the families that stay there. Our pastor suggested that we make it a tradition to deliver the tabs we'd collected every year on Taylor's birthday. After Taylor died, in 2009, we took 47 pounds of tabs and in 2010 we delivered 67 pounds. We had stayed at the RMH a lot of times and in two different states. It's something I want to continue to do every year in Taylor's memory.

I was asked to speak about Taylor's life at a meeting of the local Child Conservation League (CCL). I was thrilled to do it, because I did and still do welcome any chance to talk about her—I believe it's a part of my healing process. I was so nervous as the meeting approached, I warned them to shut me off because I have a tendency to talk too much when I get nervous. However, they loved hearing our story. I am now a member of that group.

I decided to make my wish—to donate Layla's and my favorite book to the hospital where Taylor was born and died—a reality. My plan was that any parent whose child died at that hospital would receive a copy of *Mommy, Please Don't Cry: There are No Tears in Heaven*. I hoped and prayed it would touch them as it had touched me. I talked to the nun who headed up the bereavement committee at the hospital. She estimated that 30 to 50 children a year died. If I could raise $1,100, I could purchase 100 books.

I decided to put my baking skills to work and make my dream come true. However, I was already well-known for my special filled cupcakes from a recipe a friend at work had given me. Everyone loved those cupcakes. We used to take them to Taylor's doctors and *they* loved them. It was going to take more than one bake sale to raise those kinds of funds, so in addition to baking myself, I began asking 25 family members and friends to bake items for the sale and not a single person turned me down. In fact, people started calling and emailing because they heard about it and wanted to help. We made 20 dozen filled cupcakes. I had a lot of help and Layla was right there, too. We boxed everything up for the sale that was scheduled to take place at the local bank that Friday. It started at 9:00 a.m.

We had a lot of food and business was more than brisk. Even people who said they couldn't eat sweets still helped with donations. Some just handed me money, saying they wanted to help with the books. We live in a very small community and since everyone knew about Taylor and her struggles, the response was amazing. The treats and goodies practically flew off the tables. The 20 dozen cupcakes vanished within 20 minutes. At 11:45, all that was left to clean up were empty boxes. We cleaned up and prepared for Saturday. The only problem was that all the baked goods were gone. We had nothing left and I had no idea where the stuff was going to come from to sell the next day.

When we got home, I began to count the money. I started to cry because, once again, it was overwhelmingly obvious that God's hand was on us. We had raised in just under two hours $1,094. We were $6 short of our goal.

A little while later, Deedi stopped by. She had dropped off a bunch of baked stuff for the sale earlier.

"Here," she said. "It's the $6 I owe you for the cupcakes I took this morning. I told Roger to tell you I'd bring the money by after school."

I couldn't help it and started crying again, yet I was smiling at the same time. I kept saying, "God made this possible."

Fortunately one of the local churches has a roomy, convenient kitchen with three ovens and big island in the middle. They were generous enough to let us use it as we hurriedly began baking for the next day. Assembly line fashion, Michelle, Layla, Lisa, Patti, Melissa, Heather,

Kim and I made 23 dozen more cupcakes. One mixed and poured, one was in charge of the baking. The rest of us lined up around the island and we filled and frosted like a well-oiled machine. When I called the people who had donated baked goods for the first sale and told them all the food had been sold, they offered to bake again. What a great bunch of people!

Layla wanted to help so badly—she drew pictures on little pieces of paper and said, "I will sell these at the bake sale and help raise money for the books."

She sold them before and after the sale and contributed $2.59. What a girl!

The next morning, my bakers were waiting with their goodies. There was just as much food as the day before, if not more. Everything just fell into place and it felt as if it was all being taken care of from above. Food was selling almost as fast as the day before. The filled cupcakes disappeared in 45 minutes and, just like on Friday, it was all gone by 11:45 a.m.

The man who purchased the last item spotted a framed photo of Taylor sitting on the table. He said, "How much for the picture of Taylor?"

I thought he was kidding, so I said, "Five bucks."

He said, "Here you go."

My cousin's wife, Shelly—one of my good friends—who was helping had tears in her eyes as she said, "You can't sell Taylor's picture!"

I said, "I have more pictures and I can always buy another frame. If he wants it that badly, I want him to have it."

He and his wife used to visit Taylor and called and checked on her a lot. This was yet another example of how special a kid she was to so many people. I had often told Roger that Taylor was not just our baby—she was everyone's baby. The bake sale illustrated how true that was.

When we added up the second day's proceeds, it totaled $600. That meant we could buy 150 books for the hospital. I cannot express how happy it made me. God must have had a plan for those books because not only had the book helped us, it would help others.

Deedi ordered the books. We went together to pay for them. I couldn't believe how good it felt. Not long after, half the order arrived.

When we went back to pick them up, it looked more like a thousand books and felt like they weighed that much, too. When Roger and I went back and picked up the rest of the order, the thought hit me that I had started the project and it was already almost complete.

My cousin Beth made tags to put in the books so that the people who received them would know that they were given in memory of Taylor. I knew people wouldn't know who Taylor Tumblin was but maybe they would remember her name.

I called the nun at the hospital and told her the wonderful news about the books. I think she may have been more excited than I was when I told her we were able to donate 150 books. We set up a time to deliver them. We had to figure out how we were going to get them there. Our friend Becky Jo wanted to go along to take photos, plus she wanted to meet the nun. Shelly offered her van and volunteered the use of a two-wheeled cart out of her garage.

The closer we got to the hospital, the more excited I was. Although, I had spoken to her over the phone several times, I couldn't wait to find her because I hadn't seen her since the day Taylor died. It was a wonderful reunion. I asked if I could go to the floor where Taylor was admitted that last week of her life. I wanted to see if any of the nurses who had taken care of her were working that day. To my surprise, they were. They had already heard about the books and remarked on how much they appreciated them, too.

A couple months later we received a thank you from the nun. In it she wrote that they had handed out books to some very sad parents. "Thank you very much for your dedication to making things better for other people."

It is heartbreaking that a need for the books exists, but I am so happy they have them there. I recently sent a copy of the book to a family whose two-month-old baby died. I always wonder how people will receive it, but this particular family found the same comfort between the pages as we did. They have since bought a case of the books and are giving them to other bereaved parents. Like a pebble dropped into a pond, the ripples of caring and concern grow and reach out.

† Chapter 35 †

Love Is Unconditional

If you see my mommy today
Please tell her I am fine
If you see my Daddy today
Please tell him I can play
I know how much they love me
I know how they still grieve
Still Jesus saw my need and
Brought me to His knee
He told me they were worthy
To take great care of me
Even though my time was short
He found the very best for me
My name is Taylor Tumblin
In heaven I reside
The job was so big God gave me
To teach you all one thing
I hope you learned the lesson . . .
Love Is Unconditional

Composed by Shelly Roughton
for Taylor's one-year memorial.

In the meantime, an idea began to form. Over the years, I'd kept a journal of my experiences, my highs and lows, of my love of Taylor and my awe for her journey. I wanted to spread the word about Taylor's life. She went through so much and, despite our emptiness and loss, she was such a blessing to us all. Maybe someone else would find a bit of solace in my words. Perhaps others reading her story would come to appreciate the miracle that was Taylor and understand how wonderful are the strange miracles and gifts that God gives us every day, if we choose to see them.

Roger had finally begun to show signs of healing and was as excited about my book idea as I was. We are hoping to be able to help at least one person because of this book and by sharing Taylor's story. I don't think it was just luck that Taylor had the doctors she had; I believe God sent her doctors to us. I have no doubt about that.

I have tried to put as much information as possible about everyday life and medical procedures in this book so that people will know that help is available. There are people who care and there are good doctors. Taylor was blessed with the best. Her doctors went the extra mile for Taylor and our family. I wanted to share Taylor's story so people would know that with God all things are possible. We saw His steady flow of miracles from the day we found out Taylor had Trisomy 18 and well beyond the last beat of her tiny, beautiful heart.

God had another plan for Taylor's life and, although in heaven, she was still at work. Her dad and I remained her biggest supporters as her story continued on. A teacher from our local school system had a sister who taught in the area vocational school. When she contacted me about helping her with her senior class project on Trisomy 18, I jumped at the chance. In return, she volunteered to help with the next fundraiser so we could buy books for grieving parents at additional hospitals.

I started babysitting in my home. My cousin Beth had the sweetest little girl, Rylee, who I began watching when she was five weeks old. There was a downside, however. Believe it or not, I heard that people were shocked that Beth would allow me to watch her baby after everything that had happened with Taylor. It was awful and I was shocked and hurt when I heard it. Although I didn't think Beth would let me watch her daughter if she didn't trust me, I finally confronted her about it.

"No one had better say that to me!" she responded. "I trust you and wouldn't want anyone else to keep her."

Roger thought maybe people were thinking it was too soon for me to take on babysitting. I believed I was the only one who would know if it was too soon. It was good therapy for me. I couldn't hug and kiss on Taylor, but I could on Rylee.

Shortly after that, my cousin Jana had her second child. Her son was a toddler when her baby girl was six weeks old, and I began watching both of them. In addition, I had a three-year-old boy to care for part-time. Plus, Layla was there often. The rest of the kids loved her because she was the spice in the mix and the pot was always at full-boil when she was around. Babysitting kept me busy and I often thought that Taylor would be proud of me for doing it. I have always had a lot of love to give and she would want me to share it with as many as I could.

Taylor and I sat in the house for four years and didn't leave very often. To me it was worth it. But after she died, I couldn't stay there very long without realizing how much I really missed her. That's why babysitting was the right decision for me—I could still be home, but it kept me very busy and that is what I needed.

I finally decided to go through Taylor's clothes and things. I discovered it was an easier job to get them out than when I'd packed them away. Because throughout her life people had always bought Taylor so many clothes and toys, it was almost unbelievable how many there were. I wanted to share them with others, not keep them packed away where they would be of no use to anyone. I wanted to share them with people who would truly appreciate them. It still gives me great joy to see a baby wearing one of Taylor's outfits. I just smile because I know Taylor would be happy knowing her things are being used and enjoyed by someone else.

Throughout all this, I knew I needed to stay strong. I wanted to honor Taylor by doing things to help other people in her memory. A huge number of people from our area and elsewhere were there for her and the rest of the family—so many people, always there supporting us. I have always reminded our other kids that our small community is filled with wonderful people who, when needed, are always there. The way they rallied for the bake sale was only one great example.

These same caring individuals were determined to help us through the pain of losing Taylor. They made things for us or arranged to have things made for us to help us remember her. Those gestures helped and continue to help with the pain. We met a lot of people because of Taylor and I am so thankful for them. They understood what Taylor went through and how she fought every day of her life just to stay alive. We have become the best of friends with a many of these people we never would have met if it hadn't been for Taylor.

Taylor has been gone over two years and the times I've dreamt of her, I have never seen her face, it's always just the back of her head. Until last night. Last night I had a dream that we were at the home of my cousin Diana and her husband Ron. Ron loved Taylor and in the dream he was zooming her around like an airplane. She was smiling ear to ear and laughing out loud. When I woke up, I was all smiles myself. What a great feeling!

Decades may pass and our lives will go on. And although we will gather as a family and laugh together and talk together. . .a child who dies leaves a gap that can never be filled. Taylor was sent to us from God, even though He called her home at such an early age. She did it all, despite what we were told: she wouldn't survive; she wouldn't leave the hospital; she would never talk; she would never go to school. Her success was all in His plan. She wasn't supposed to be here one day. What a miracle she was.

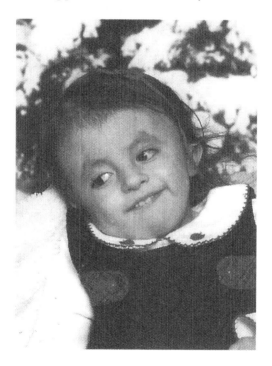

Taylor

The strongest person I know
Was four when she died.
And even though we miss her,
She can finally shine.
She can run and play and do
. . . All the things she couldn't on earth.

She can laugh and sing
And jump and twirl,
Just like any other little girl.
She was always so special,
The apple of so many eyes,
Just seeing her face would make you smile.
She fought a hard battle,
And won for four years. Against all odds,
She was our little hero.
The Lord brought her home in 2009,
But she'll remain in our hearts
Until the end of time ♥

Allyson Brown

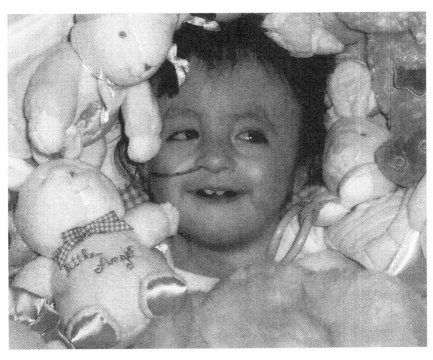

Taylor (with poem)

Abby and Taylor

Deedi and Taylor

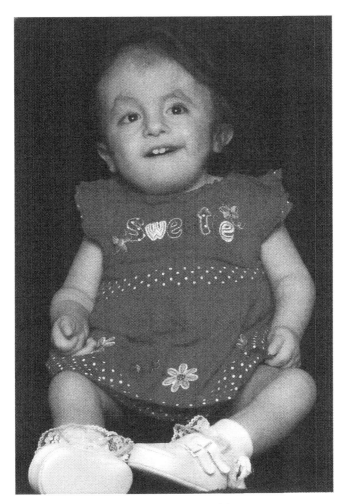

Taylor at 3 years old

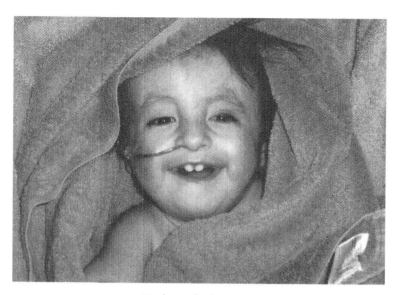

Taylor at bath time

Taylor with sister Danielle

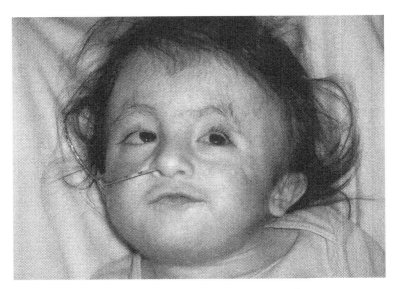

Taylor looking like she's up to no good

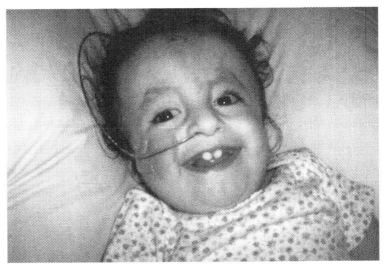

What a happy girl

Taylor thinking "Who are you?"

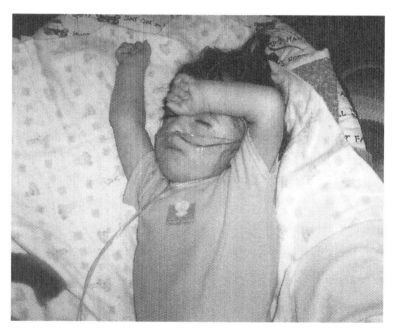

Exhausted little Taylor

Taylor and Layla—best friends

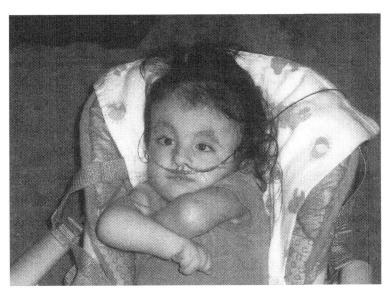

Taylor with an attitude

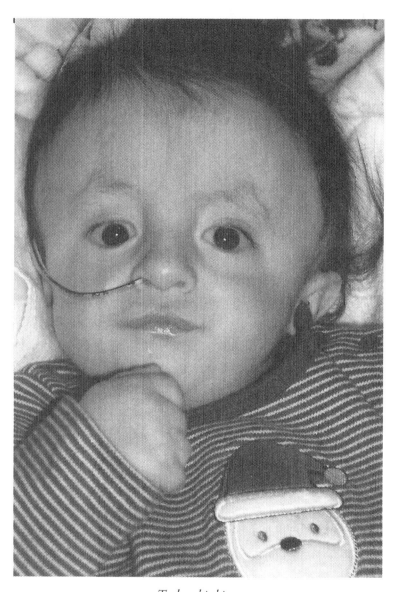

Taylor thinking

Taylor and Layla

Taylor and Layla

Layla pushing Taylor in a doll stroller

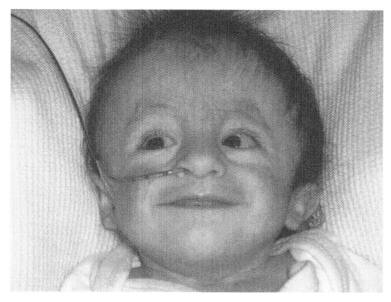

Million-dollar smile

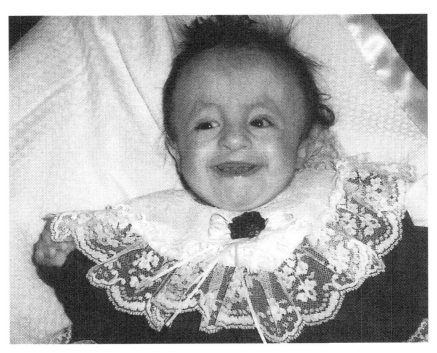

Taylor in one of her Christmas dresses